Computer Networking
Interview Questions and Answers

X.Y. Wang

Contents

6 Guru   **123**

Chapter 1

Introduction

Welcome to "Computer Networking: Interview Questions and Answers". As we continue to rely on computer networks to communicate, exchange information, and access resources, understanding the intricacies of networking becomes increasingly important. In this book, we will explore a wide range of topics related to computer networking, from the fundamental concepts to the cutting-edge technologies.

The goal of this book is to provide an extensive collection of interview questions and answers that will help you succeed in your career in the field of computer networking. Whether you are a student seeking an entry-level position or a seasoned professional looking to advance your career, you will find this book to be an invaluable resource.

"Computer Networking: Interview Questions and Answers" is structured into five sections, each covering a different level of complexity: Basic, Intermediate, Advanced, Expert, and Guru. This organization allows you to easily navigate the content and find the information you need, based on your current skill level and the requirements of the position you are seeking.

In the Basic section, we cover the foundations of computer networking, including the OSI model, IP addressing, and network devices such as switches and routers. We then progress to the Intermediate section, where we delve into topics such as VLANs, routing protocols, and network security concepts like firewalls.

The Advanced section introduces more sophisticated topics such as network virtualization, encryption, and intrusion detection systems. In the Expert section, you will encounter high-level discussions on network design, management, and security, as well as emerging technologies like 5G and edge computing.

Finally, the Guru section covers cutting-edge topics such as Intent-Based Networking, quantum computing, and advanced network analysis techniques. These questions and answers will challenge your understanding of the field and help you stay ahead of the curve.

Throughout the book, the questions and answers are designed to be concise, clear, and to-the-point, allowing you to quickly grasp the key concepts and principles. Additionally, the questions are derived from real-life interviews and reflect the challenges and scenarios you may encounter in your networking career.

"Computer Networking: Interview Questions and Answers" is not only a comprehensive guide for job seekers but also a valuable reference for networking professionals seeking to expand their knowledge and stay current with the latest advancements in the field. With this book as your guide, you'll be well-equipped to tackle the challenges of the ever-evolving world of computer networking.

So, without further ado, let's dive into the fascinating world of computer networking and prepare you for your next interview and networking challenge!

Chapter 2

Basic

2.1 What is the OSI model and why is it important in computer networking?

The OSI (Open Systems Interconnection) model is a conceptual framework that describes the communication functions of a telecommunication or computer system. It consists of seven layers, each with a specific role in the process of transmitting data between networked devices.

The seven layers of the OSI model are as follows:

1. Physical layer: This layer defines the physical characteristics of the network such as the cable type, connector type, and data transmission rate.

2. Data link layer: This layer is responsible for framing data and performing error detection and correction.

3. Network layer: This layer is responsible for routing data between multiple networks and ensuring that it reaches its intended destination.

4. Transport layer: This layer regulates the flow of data and provides

end-to-end error recovery and flow control.

5. Session layer: This layer establishes and maintains connections between devices and manages the transfer of data.

6. Presentation layer: This layer formats data for presentation to the application layer.

7. Application layer: This layer provides network services to applications and enables them to communicate with each other.

The OSI model is important in computer networking because it provides a standard for communication between different vendors and platforms. With a standardized model, networking equipment and software can be developed independently and still work together seamlessly. It also allows for troubleshooting and problem-solving at each layer of the model, making it easier to identify and fix issues in the network.

Additionally, the OSI model provides a common language for network engineers and administrators. When discussing networking concepts and issues, everyone involved can reference the same layered architecture, making it easier to communicate and understand each other.

Overall, the OSI model is a crucial component of computer networking and has played an important role in standardizing communication protocols and facilitating efficient data transmission.

2.2 What is the difference between a LAN, MAN, and WAN?

LAN, MAN, and WAN are three types of computer networks that differ in their geographical coverage and the number of nodes they can support.

A LAN (Local Area Network) is a type of network that covers a small geographic area, typically within a single building or a campus. LANs are used to connect devices such as computers, printers, and servers, and enable them to share resources such as data, applications, and peripherals. Examples of LANs include home networks, school networks, and office networks. LANs can support up to thousands of nodes, and they typically use Ethernet, Wi-Fi, or a combination of both as their primary communication protocol.

A MAN (Metropolitan Area Network) is a type of network that covers a larger geographic area than a LAN, typically spanning a city or a metropolitan area. MANs are used to connect multiple LANs in different locations, and enable them to share resources and communicate with each other. MANs can support up to tens of thousands of nodes, and they typically use technologies such as ATM, FDDI, or Metro Ethernet as their primary communication protocol.

A WAN (Wide Area Network) is a type of network that covers a large geographic area, typically spanning multiple cities, countries, or even continents. WANs are used to connect multiple MANs or LANs in different locations, and enable them to communicate with each other over long distances. WANs can support millions of nodes, and they typically use technologies such as leased lines, satellite links, or the Internet as their primary communication protocol.

In summary, the main differences between LAN, MAN, and WAN are their geographical coverage, the number of nodes they can support, and the communication technologies they use. While LANs are localized networks that cover a small area and typically use Ethernet or Wi-Fi, MANs cover a larger area and use technologies such as ATM or Metro Ethernet. WANs cover a large area and use communication technologies such as leased lines or satellite links to enable long-distance communication between different LANs or MANs.

2.3   Can you define and differentiate between TCP and UDP protocols?

TCP and UDP are both transport layer protocols that are used to transfer data over a network. However, they have some distinct differences that make them suitable for different types of applications.

TCP, or Transmission Control Protocol, is a reliable, connection-oriented protocol. This means that it establishes a connection between two devices before transmitting data and ensures that all data packets are received in the correct order. TCP is responsible for error correction, flow control, and congestion control to ensure that data is delivered without loss or duplication. This makes TCP ideal for applications where accuracy and completeness are critical, such as file transfers, email, and web browsing.

For example, when you download a file from a website, your browser uses TCP to establish a connection to the server before transferring the entire file, ensuring that all packets are received and retransmitted without error until the file is completely downloaded.

UDP, or User Datagram Protocol, is a faster, connectionless protocol that does not provide error correction, flow control, or congestion control. This means that data packets may be lost or duplicated during transmission, and there is no guarantee that they arrive in the correct order. UDP is ideal for applications where speed is more important than accuracy, such as video conferencing, online gaming, and real-time streaming.

For example, when you play an online game, your device uses UDP to send data packets to the game server, prioritizing speed over accuracy. If some packets are lost on the way, the game server will continue to provide a real-time experience without waiting for retransmission of missing packets.

To summarize, TCP provides a reliable and accurate communication while UDP offers a faster but less reliable service. The choice between TCP and UDP depends on the specific requirements of an application.

2.4   What are IP addresses and how are they classified?

An IP address is a unique numerical identifier that is assigned to each device connected to a computer network that uses the Internet Protocol for communication. It serves as a routing and identification address that identifies the network and host of a device on the internet.

IP addresses are divided into two versions: IPv4 and IPv6. IPv4 addresses are 32-bit numbers that are divided into four octets, each of which ranges from 0 to 255. IPv4 addresses are written in dotted-decimal notation, such as 192.168.1.1. IPv6 addresses are 128-bit numbers that are written in hexadecimal notation, such as 2001:0db8:85a3:0000:0000:8a2e:0370:7334.

IP addresses are further divided into classes, which are based on the size of the network and the number of hosts that can be connected to it. There are five classes of IP addresses: A, B, C, D, and E.

Class A IP addresses are used for large networks with a large number of hosts. The first bit of a Class A IP address is set to 0, and the next 7 bits represent the network identifier, which leaves 24 bits for the host identifier. This allows for up to 126 networks and over 16 million hosts per network.

Class B IP addresses are used for medium-sized networks. The first two bits of a Class B IP address are set to 10, and the next 14 bits represent the network identifier, which leaves 16 bits for the host identifier. This allows for up to 16,384 networks and 65,534 hosts per network.

Class C IP addresses are used for small networks. The first three bits of a Class C IP address are set to 110, and the next 21 bits represent the network identifier, which leaves 8 bits for the host identifier. This allows for up to 2 million networks and 254 hosts per network.

Class D IP addresses are used for multicast addresses, which are used to send messages to a group of devices on the network. The first four bits of a Class D IP address are set to 1110.

Class E IP addresses are reserved for experimental use and the first four bits of a Class E IP address are set to 1111.

In summary, IP addresses are unique numeric identifiers that identify devices on a computer network. They are classified into different classes based on the number of hosts and networks that can be connected to it, with Class A being the largest and Class E being reserved for experimental use.

2.5   What is a subnet mask, and why is it used in IP addressing?

In an IP network, subnetting is the practice of dividing a single network into smaller subnetworks, called subnets. A subnet is a logical division of an IP network that can allow different physical networks to share the same address space. In order to create subnets, a subnet mask is used.

A subnet mask is a 32-bit value used to divide an IP address into two parts, the network address and the host address. The subnet mask is used by the network devices to determine which part of an IP address is the network portion and which part is the host portion. It is typically represented using the dotted decimal notation, which consists of four numbers separated by dots. Each number represents eight bits, and the value of each number can be any value from 0 to 255.

For example, consider an IP address of 192.168.1.100 with a subnet mask of 255.255.255.0. In this case, the first three numbers, 192.168.1, represent the network portion, and the last number, 100, represents the host portion. The subnet mask of 255.255.255.0 indicates that the first three octets are the network portion and the last octet is the host portion.

The use of subnets and subnet masks provides several benefits to IP networks. One of the primary benefits is that it allows network administrators to conserve IP addresses. By dividing a larger network into smaller subnets, each subnet can have its own set of IP addresses, which can be more efficiently allocated to devices within that subnet. Additionally, subnets can be used to control network traffic by isolating devices within a certain portion of the network.

In conclusion, subnet masks are used in IP addressing to divide a single IP network into smaller subnets. They help conserve IP addresses and control network traffic by dividing the network into smaller logical units.

2.6   How does a network switch differ from a network hub?

A network switch and a network hub are both networking devices that connect multiple devices in a local area network (LAN). However, they differ in their functionality and the way they handle data transmission.

A hub is a basic networking device that allows multiple devices to communicate with each other by broadcasting all data packets to every device on the network. When a device transmits data to the hub, the hub broadcasts the data to all the devices on the network. This means that every device on the network sees all of the traffic, regardless of whether it is intended for them. As the number of devices on the network increases, the amount of network traffic also increases, which can lead to congestion and slow network performance.

In contrast, a switch is a more advanced networking device that only sends data to the intended recipient. When a switch receives data from a device, it reads the destination MAC address of the packet and forwards it only to the device that is supposed to receive it. This creates a more efficient flow of traffic on the network because there is less unnecessary traffic being transmitted. Switches also have the capability to create multiple virtual LANs (VLANs), which can segment network traffic and improve network performance.

To illustrate the difference, consider a scenario where several devices on a network are transmitting data simultaneously. In a hub-based network, when one device transmits data, all the other devices receive the data, even if it is not intended for them. This creates a lot of unnecessary traffic on the network, which can lead to congestion and network performance issues. In contrast, in a switch-based network, when a device transmits data, the switch reads the destination MAC address of the packet and forwards it only to the intended recipient. This creates a more efficient flow of traffic on the network and reduces unnecessary congestion.

In summary, the main difference between a network switch and a network hub is that a switch is a more advanced device that can selectively transmit data to the intended recipient, while a hub broadcasts all data to all devices on the network.

2.7 What are the roles of routers and switches in a computer network?

Routers and switches are essential networking components that play a vital role in the overall functioning and management of a computer network. While they share some similarities in terms of their function, they have distinct roles to play in transmitting data and connecting devices.

Routers are devices that sit at the edge of a network and are responsible for directing traffic between different networks. They use routing algorithms to determine the best path for data to travel based on factors such as network congestion, proximity, and reliability. Routers are also able to filter traffic based on specific rules or policies, allowing administrators to control which devices or applications have access to the network. For example, when you connect to the internet from your home router, it acts as a gateway, directing your internet traffic to the appropriate destination.

Switches, on the other hand, are devices that are used to connect different devices within a network, enabling them to communicate with each other. Switches operate at the data-link layer of the network, and their primary function is to route data packets between hardware devices by reading their MAC addresses. Switches use a technique called forward-table lookup, where they store a table of MAC addresses of devices connected to the switch and the port associated with each MAC address, enabling quick and efficient data routing.

To illustrate the roles of routers and switches, consider a typical corporate network consisting of multiple departments spread across different floors of a building. In this scenario, each department has several devices such as computers, printers, and servers that need to communicate with each other. To enable this communication, switches are used to connect the devices within each department, while routers are used to connect the different departments, ensuring that data can be transmitted across the network between different floors.

In summary, routers and switches are both critical components of modern computer networks, and they play different but complementary roles in network communication. Routers enable data exchange between different networks and provide an essential layer of security, while switches facilitate communication between devices within a network, allowing for efficient routing of data packets.

2.8   Can you explain the difference between unicast, multicast, and broadcast?

In computer networking, communication between devices happens in different ways, and unicast, multicast, and broadcast are three common methods used to send data packets among devices.

Unicast is a one-to-one transmission method, where a single packet is sent from a sender to a specific receiver on the network. The receiver's address is the only one included in the packet header, which means that only that receiver can see and process the packet. Unicast is the most common communication method used in computer networks. For example, when you browse a website, your device sends unicast packets to the server, and the server sends unicast packets back to your device.

Multicast, on the other hand, is a one-to-many transmission method, where a single packet is sent from the sender to a group of devices that subscribe to that particular multicast group address. When a device sends a multicast packet, it explicitly identifies the multicast group address in the packet header, and all devices that have subscribed to that multicast group address will receive and process the packet. Multicast is commonly used in multimedia applications, such as online streaming, where a single stream of data is distributed to many devices at once. For instance, when devices stream music or video from a service, the service sends the stream as multicast packets to all the devices that have subscribed to that particular stream.

Finally, broadcast is a one-to-all transmission method, where a single packet is sent from the sender to all devices on the local network. In broadcast, the destination address is not a specific device, but instead a broadcast address that represents all devices on the network. When a device sends a broadcast packet, all devices on the local network receive and process the packet. Broadcast is typically used for network discovery or network management tasks. For instance, when a device joins a network or acquires an IP address, it broadcasts a packet to all devices on the network to inform them of its presence.

In summary, unicast is a one-to-one transmission method, multicast is a one-to-many transmission method, and broadcast is a one-to-all transmission method. These three methods have different purposes and use cases, and understanding their differences is essential for building and managing computer networks.

2.9 What is the role of the Domain Name System (DNS) in networking?

The Domain Name System (DNS) plays a crucial role in networking, as it provides a standardized way to convert human-readable domain names into machine-readable IP addresses. Every device connected to the internet has a unique IP address, which is a numerical identifier used to locate and communicate with other devices. However, remembering and typing in IP addresses is difficult for humans, and IP addresses can also be dynamic and change frequently.

DNS solves this problem by providing a hierarchical naming system for domain names, such as "google.com" or "facebook.com". When a user enters a domain name into a web browser or other network application, the application sends a DNS query to a DNS resolver, asking for the IP address associated with that domain name. The resolver then contacts a DNS server to obtain the IP address and returns it to the application, which can then use the IP address to establish the desired connection.

DNS operates using a distributed architecture, with multiple levels of servers and caches that help to improve performance and reliability. At the highest level are the root servers, which are responsible for maintaining a database of all top-level domains (e.g. .com, .gov, .net, etc.). Below the root servers are the top-level domain (TLD) servers, which are responsible for managing the domain names for a particular TLD (e.g. .com). At the lowest level are the authoritative name servers, which are responsible for maintaining the DNS records for individual domain names.

When a DNS query is made, the resolver first checks its cache to see if it already has the IP address for the requested domain name. If not, it contacts one of the root servers to obtain the IP address for the appropriate TLD server. The TLD server then returns the IP address for the authoritative name server for the requested domain name, and the resolver can then contact the authoritative name server to obtain the actual IP address for the domain name.

In addition to translating domain names into IP addresses, DNS also provides other types of information, such as mail server information and security settings. DNS is a critical component of the internet infrastructure, and its functionality and reliability are essential for the proper operation of many network applications and services.

2.10   How do MAC addresses play a role in computer networking?

In computer networking, MAC (Media Access Control) addresses play an important role in identifying devices on a network. A MAC address is a unique identifier assigned to each device's network interface controller (NIC) by the manufacturer. It consists of six pairs of hexadecimal characters separated by colons, such as 00:1A:2B:3C:4D:5E.

MAC addresses operate at the data link layer of the OSI model and are used by network devices, such as switches and routers, to forward packets across the network. When a device wants to transmit data to another device on the same network, it first checks the destination MAC address of the packet. If the destination MAC address is not in the device's ARP (Address Resolution Protocol) cache, it sends out an ARP request to broadcast on the network, asking for the MAC address of the device with the specified IP address. Once the device receives a response from the device with the matching IP address, it adds the MAC address to its ARP cache and can then send the packet directly to that device using its MAC address.

MAC addresses are also used by switches to build their forwarding tables, which are used to determine the path a packet should take to reach its destination. When a switch receives a packet, it checks the destination MAC address of the packet and looks it up in its forwarding table. If the MAC address is in the table, the switch forwards the packet to the corresponding port. If not, the switch broadcasts the packet to all ports, except the port it received the packet from, in order to learn which port the device with the matching MAC address is connected to. Once the switch learns the location of the device, it adds the MAC address to its forwarding table for future reference.

In summary, MAC addresses play a crucial role in computer networking by providing a unique identifier for each device on a network. They allow devices to communicate with each other and enable switches to build their forwarding tables, which are used to efficiently forward packets across the network.

2.11   What is DHCP, and why is it important for managing IP addresses?

DHCP stands for Dynamic Host Configuration Protocol. It is a network protocol that enables a server to automatically assign an IP address and other network configuration parameters to devices on a network.

In traditional networks, network administrators would assign IP addresses manually. This can be time-consuming and error-prone, especially in large networks. DHCP automates this process, freeing up administrators' time to focus on more critical tasks.

DHCP operates on a client-server model. When a device connects to a network, it sends a broadcast message requesting an IP address. The DHCP server responds with an available IP address and other configuration information, such as subnet mask, default gateway, and DNS server. The device then configures its network settings with the assigned IP address and other configuration details.

The benefits of DHCP include:

1. IP address management: DHCP ensures that IP addresses are assigned efficiently and eliminates the risk of human error. It also simplifies the process of moving devices between different network

segments.

2. Scalability: DHCP is well-suited for large networks where manual IP address assignment is not practical.

3. Centralized management: DHCP enables centralized management and configuration of network devices.

4. Reduced network traffic: DHCP reduces network traffic by eliminating unnecessary broadcasts, which improves network performance.

Overall, DHCP plays a critical role in managing IP addresses in modern computer networks. Without DHCP, network administration would be more complex, and network performance and security could be impacted.

2.12 Can you explain the basic concept of Network Address Translation (NAT)?

Network Address Translation (NAT) is a technique used to facilitate communication between devices in different IP address spaces. It is commonly implemented in routers and firewalls to allow multiple devices on a local network to share a single public IP address. NAT operates by changing the IP address in the header of each IP packet that passes through it.

There are several types of NAT, but the most commonly used is called "source NAT" or "SNAT". In SNAT, the router or firewall modifies the source IP address of outgoing packets to its own public IP address, and keeps track of the changes in a translation table. When a response is received, the router consults the translation table to determine which local device the response should be forwarded to.

For example, consider a small office network consisting of several devices connected to a router with a public IP address of 203.0.113.1. Each device on the local network has a private IP address in the range of 192.168.1.0/24. When a device on the local network wants to access a website, it sends a request with its own private IP address as the source address. The router changes the source address to its own public IP address and forwards the request to the website. The website responds to the public IP address, and the router uses the translation table to forward the response to the correct local device based on its private IP address.

NAT also provides a level of security by hiding the private IP addresses of devices on a local network from the public Internet. This helps prevent unauthorized access to devices on the network, and reduces the risk of targeted attacks. However, NAT can cause issues with certain types of applications that require direct access to the Internet, such as peer-to-peer file sharing or online gaming. In these cases, special configurations or workarounds may be necessary to allow the applications to function correctly.

2.13 What is the function of a firewall in a computer network?

A firewall is a network security device that monitors and filters incoming and outgoing network traffic based on an organization's previously established security policies. The primary function of a firewall is to block unauthorized or malicious traffic from entering or leaving the network.

Firewalls work in various ways to protect a network from cyber-attacks. One way is by creating a barrier between the internal network and the internet, preventing malicious traffic from entering the network. Another way is by analyzing each data packet that passes through it and allowing or blocking traffic based on pre-configured rules.

Firewalls can be implemented in various forms, such as hardware, software or a combination of both. Hardware firewalls are devices that are installed at the network's edge, between the internal network and the internet. They are designed to protect the entire network from external threats. Software firewalls, on the other hand, are installed on individual systems and are designed to protect that specific system from external threats.

For example, imagine a company has a website that can be accessed by anyone on the internet. Without a firewall in place, hackers can send packets to the company's web servers to try and gain unauthorized access to sensitive information. However, with a firewall in place, the packets will be analyzed, and any malicious traffic will be blocked, preventing the hackers from gaining access to the company's information.

In summary, the function of a firewall in a computer network is to provide security by filtering incoming and outgoing network traffic and blocking any unauthorized or malicious traffic from accessing the network.

2.14   What are the main types of network topologies, and how do they differ?

A network topology refers to the physical or logical layout of a network. The main types are:

1. Bus Topology: A bus topology consists of a single cable connecting all devices in the network. Each device is connected to the cable via a tap or connector. This type of topology is commonly used in small networks.

2. Star Topology: A star topology consists of a central device (such as a hub or switch) connected to each device in the network. All communication between devices must pass through the central device. This type of network is commonly used in larger networks.

3. Ring Topology: A ring topology consists of each device connected to two other devices, creating a ring shape. Each device in the network receives and transmits data. This type of topology is not commonly used due to its vulnerability to failure.

4. Mesh Topology: A mesh topology consists of each device connected to every other device in the network, creating a fully interconnected network. Data can be transmitted directly between devices without passing through a central device. This type of topology is commonly used in large networks where high reliability and availability are required.

Each type of topology has its own advantages and disadvantages. Bus topology is easy to install and requires less cable, but a fault in the main cable can bring down the entire network. Star topology is easy to manage and allows for easy addition or removal of devices, but all communication must pass through the central device. Ring topology is efficient and provides equal access to all devices, but a fault in one device can bring down the entire network. Mesh topology provides high reliability and availability, but can be expensive and difficult to manage.

In summary, the choice of network topology depends on the specific requirements of the network, such as size, cost, reliability, and manageability.

2.15 What are the differences between network cables, such as twisted-pair, coaxial, and fiber-optic cables?

Network cables can be classified into different types based on the technology they employ for data transmission. The major types of network cables are twisted-pair, coaxial, and fiber-optic cables. The major differences between these cable types can be found in terms of their construction, the transmission speeds they support, the maximum length of cable that can be used, and their resistance to electromagnetic interference (EMI).

Twisted-pair cables are commonly used in Ethernet networks. They consist of two insulated copper wires twisted together in a helical pattern. These wires are twisted to reduce electromagnetic interference and crosstalk between the wires. Twisted-pair cables are further classified into two types: unshielded twisted-pair (UTP) and shielded twisted-pair (STP) cables. UTP cables are the most commonly used network cables in Ethernet networks. They provide good transmission speeds for short cable runs, but the maximum distance at which data can be transmitted is limited to around 100 meters. STP cables are designed to provide additional protection from EMI, making them suitable for environments with high levels of interference.

Coaxial cables consist of a copper wire conductor surrounded by an insulating layer, a metallic shield, and a plastic or rubber jacket. The copper wire is used to transmit data, while the metallic shield provides protection against EMI. Coaxial cables support higher transmission speeds than twisted-pair cables, making them suitable for cable television (CATV) networks and high-speed internet connections. Coaxial cables have a maximum transmission distance of around 500 meters.

Fiber-optic cables are based on the principle of transmitting data using light pulses. They consist of a core made of glass or plastic fibers, surrounded by a cladding layer and a protective jacket. Fiber-optic cables support the highest transmission speeds of all network cables, making them suitable for high-bandwidth applications such as data centers, telecommunication networks, and high-speed internet connections. Fiber-optic cables also have the longest transmission distance, up to several kilometers. They are resistant to EMI and have a higher level of security as they are difficult to tap into.

In conclusion, the choice of network cable will depend on the specific application requirements, such as transmission speed, distance, and EMI considerations. Each cable type has its own advantages and disadvantages, and network engineers need to carefully evaluate and select the appropriate cable type based on the particular use case.

2.16   Can you explain the concept of a Virtual Private Network (VPN) and its uses?

A Virtual Private Network (VPN) is a technology that provides a secure and private communication channel between two or more devices over the Internet. It allows users to access network resources or browse the web securely and anonymously using an encrypted tunnel.

The basic idea behind a VPN is to create a secure tunnel between two devices which encrypts all data passing through it. This ensures that even if someone intercepts the data, they will not be able to read it, as it will be encrypted.

A VPN can be used for various purposes, such as protecting user privacy, bypassing censorship and firewalls, or accessing resources on a remote network. Here are some examples of how a VPN is used:

1. Remote Access: VPNs can be used by employees to access their company's network remotely. This is especially useful for employees who work from home, or when traveling. The VPN helps to keep data secure, even when accessed from an unsecured network.

2. Secure Browsing: VPNs can be used to browse the web securely and privately. The encrypted tunnel ensures that user data is protected from interception or snooping by ISPs, governments, or hackers.

3. Geo-restricted Content: VPNs can be used to bypass geo-restrictions put in place by content providers. For example, if a user wants to access Netflix in a country where it is not available, they can use a VPN to connect to a server in a country where it is available.

4. Torrenting: VPNs can be used to download torrents without revealing the user's IP address. This helps to protect the user's privacy and prevent them from being tracked by copyright trolls.

5. Public Wi-Fi: VPNs can be used to protect users when using public Wi-Fi networks. Public Wi-Fi networks are often unsecured, making users vulnerable to hacking and snooping. A VPN encrypts all data passing through the network, keeping it secure.

In conclusion, a VPN is a powerful tool that provides secure and private communication over the Internet. It can be used for a variety of purposes, including remote access, secure browsing, bypassing geo-restrictions, and protecting user privacy.

2.17 What is the purpose of a network protocol, and can you name some common ones?

A network protocol is a set of rules that govern the communication between devices in a computer network. These rules define how data is transmitted over the network, including the format of the data, the order in which it is transmitted, and the actions taken in response to certain events.

The purpose of a network protocol is to provide a standard way for devices to communicate with each other. This enables devices and applications from different vendors to work together seamlessly, and ensures that data is transmitted reliably and securely. Network protocols help to facilitate the efficient and effective flow of information across the network.

Some common network protocols include:

1. Transmission Control Protocol (TCP): This is the most widely used protocol on the internet, and is responsible for creating connections between devices and for reliably transmitting data between them. TCP is a connection-oriented protocol, meaning it establishes a connection before transmitting data, and it ensures that data is correctly received and retransmits any lost packets.

2. Internet Protocol (IP): This is the protocol responsible for routing packets across the internet. IP is a connectionless protocol, meaning it transmits packets of data without establishing a connection with the recipient first. IP defines the format of the packets, including the source and destination addresses, and provides a mechanism for routing packets to the correct destination.

3. User Datagram Protocol (UDP): This is a simpler, connectionless protocol that is used for applications that do not require the reliability features of TCP. UDP does not provide any guarantees that data will be reliably transmitted, but it is faster and more efficient for applications that can tolerate some loss of data.

4. HyperText Transfer Protocol (HTTP): This is the protocol used to transfer web pages over the internet. HTTP defines the format of the request and response messages exchanged between web servers and web browsers, and provides a way for clients to request resources from servers and for servers to respond with the requested data.

5. Simple Mail Transfer Protocol (SMTP): This is the protocol used to transmit email messages across the internet. SMTP is a connection-oriented protocol that allows mail servers to exchange email messages with each other. It defines the format of email messages and provides a way for mail servers to verify the identity of the sender and receiver of the email.

2.18 What are the advantages and disadvantages of using wireless networks over wired networks?

Wireless networks and wired networks are two different types of computer networks. Wired networks use physical cables (such as Ethernet cables) to connect devices, while wireless networks use radio waves to connect devices (such as Wi-Fi networks).

Advantages of Wireless Networks:

1. Mobility: One of the main advantages of wireless networks is mobility. Devices connected to a wireless network can move around freely within the range of the network without the need for physical cables.

2. Convenience: Wireless networks are convenient as they eliminate the need for physical cables, which can be messy and cumbersome to deal with. Devices connected to a wireless network also don't need to be close to a physical port or cable.

3. Flexibility: Wireless networks are flexible, making it easy to add new devices to the network without needing to run new cables. This is particularly useful for large or complex networks where adding new cables could be difficult.

4. Lower cost: In general, wireless networks are cheaper to set up than wired networks. The cost of running cables and installing physical ports and switches can be significant, particularly for larger networks.

Disadvantages of Wireless Networks:

1. Security: Wireless networks are inherently less secure than wired networks. Radio waves can be intercepted by anyone within range, making it easier for hackers to gain access to the network. This can be mitigated using encryption and other security measures, but wireless networks are still generally less secure than wired networks.

2. Slower speeds: Wireless networks are generally slower than wired networks. This is because radio waves have limited bandwidth and can be affected by environmental factors such as distance and inter-

ference.

3. Unreliability: Wireless networks are less reliable than wired networks. Radio waves can be disrupted by physical obstacles such as walls, and interference from other electronic devices can also cause problems.

4. Limited range: The range of a wireless network is limited. While it is possible to extend the range of a wireless network using repeaters or other devices, this can be problematic for large or complex networks.

In conclusion, wireless networks offer flexibility, mobility, and lower cost but are less secure, slower, less reliable and have a limited range compared to wired networks. Therefore, the choice of network type depends on the specific needs of the user or organization.

2.19   What is the difference between a network's bandwidth and latency?

In computer networking, bandwidth and latency are two important concepts that are often used to describe the performance of a network.

Bandwidth refers to the amount of data that can be transmitted over a network in a certain amount of time. It is usually measured in bits or bytes per second (bps or Bps). Bandwidth is affected by factors such as the physical limitations of the network, the number of devices using the network, and the type of data being transmitted.

For example, imagine you are downloading a large file from the internet. The higher the bandwidth of your internet connection, the faster the file will be downloaded. If your internet connection has a bandwidth of 100 Mbps, it means that you can download 100 megabits of data per second.

Latency, on the other hand, refers to the delay that occurs when data is transmitted over a network. It is usually measured in milliseconds (ms) and represents the amount of time it takes for a packet of data to travel from one point on the network to another. Latency is affected by factors such as the distance between the devices on the network, the number of devices on the network, and the quality of the network infrastructure.

For example, imagine you are playing an online game that requires a fast response time. The lower the latency of your network, the better your game performance will be. If your network latency is 50 ms, it means that there is a 50 millisecond delay between when you perform an action in the game and when that action is reflected in the game itself.

To summarize, bandwidth determines how much data can be transmitted over a network, while latency determines how quickly data can be transmitted over a network. Both are important factors in evaluating the performance of a network, and optimizing them can help to ensure that data is transmitted efficiently and effectively.

2.20   How do error detection and correction work in data communication?

Error detection and correction techniques are crucial in data communication networks to ensure the reliable delivery of data. Without these techniques, errors in transmitted data can occur and negatively impact the accuracy and integrity of the communication.

Error detection techniques involve adding extra bits to the transmitted data to detect errors that may occur during transmission. These extra bits, known as parity bits or checksums, are calculated based on the data being transmitted and are appended to the data. When the data is received at the destination, the parity bits or checksums are recalculated and compared with the original ones. If any discrepancies are found, errors in the data transmission are detected and corrective measures can be taken.

There are different error detection techniques, but one commonly used one is the cyclic redundancy check (CRC). In CRC, a polynomial is used to generate a checksum that is appended to the data. At the receiving end, the same polynomial is used to recalculate the checksum, and if it does not match the one originally transmitted, an error is detected.

Error correction techniques, on the other hand, allow for the correction of errors that are detected in transmitted data. These techniques are especially important in networks where re-transmission of data is not feasible due to latency or time constraints. One commonly used error correction technique is forward error correction (FEC), where redundant information is added to the transmitted data to enable the receiver to correct errors without requesting a re-transmission.

In FEC, the sender adds extra bits to the original data based on an encoding algorithm. At the receiving end, the receiver uses a decoding algorithm to identify and correct errors. The amount of redundancy added depends on the level of protection required, and the trade-off between the amount of redundancy and the potential benefits in terms of error correction.

In conclusion, error detection and correction techniques are crucial in data communication networks to ensure reliable transmission of data. Error detection techniques enable the detection of errors, while error correction techniques enable the correction of errors without requiring re-transmission of data. Without these techniques, errors in transmitted data can lead to poor performance and inaccurate communication.

Chapter 3

Intermediate

3.1 Can you explain the concept of a VLAN and its benefits in network management?

A VLAN (Virtual Local Area Network) is a logical group of network devices that can communicate with each other as if they were on the same physical network, even if they are located on different network segments. VLANs are created by assigning a unique identifier, called a VLAN ID, to a group of devices, thus forming a separate broadcast domain.

The key benefits of using VLANs in network management are:

1. Segmentation: VLANs allow network administrators to segment a large and complex network into smaller, more manageable broadcast domains. This helps to reduce network congestion, improve network performance, and increase security.

2. Security: VLANs provide a layer of security by allowing administrators to isolate traffic from specific devices or groups of devices. This makes it more difficult for unauthorized users to access critical data and systems.

3. Flexibility: VLANs are very flexible and can be easily reconfigured
to adapt to changing network requirements. For example, if a new
department is added to an organization, it can be assigned its own
VLAN without disrupting the rest of the network.

4. Cost Savings: VLANs can help to reduce costs by allowing multiple
logical networks to share the same physical infrastructure. This eliminates the need for separate physical networks, which can be costly
to install and maintain.

For example, let's assume an organization has three departments:
Sales, Marketing, and Human Resources. Each of these departments
has its own set of network devices, such as computers, printers, and
servers. Without VLANs, all these devices would be connected to
the same physical network, creating a large and complex broadcast
domain. This could lead to network congestion, performance issues,
and security risks.

By using VLANs, the network administrator can assign each department its own VLAN, thus creating separate broadcast domains for
each department. This allows each department to communicate with
each other as if they were on the same physical network, while also
providing a layer of security and reducing network congestion. Additionally, if a new department is added to the organization, it can
be easily assigned its own VLAN without disrupting the rest of the
network.

3.2   How do the sliding window protocol and flow control mechanisms work in networking?

The sliding window protocol and flow control mechanisms are essential features of networking that ensure efficient and reliable data
transmission between devices. In this answer, we will discuss how
these mechanisms work and their importance in network operations.

Sliding Window Protocol

The sliding window protocol is a technique for sending multiple data packets across a network without waiting for an acknowledgement from the receiver after sending each packet. It allows the sender to transmit a certain number of packets, known as the window size, before waiting for an acknowledgement. The receiver sends an acknowledgement packet to the sender for each packet received correctly. The sender can then move the window forward and transmit additional packets.

The sliding window protocol ensures efficient utilization of the network resources and minimizes the transmission overhead. It also provides a mechanism for error detection and recovery. If a packet is lost or damaged during transmission, the receiver will not send an acknowledgment to the sender. The sender will then detect the lost packet and retransmit it.

For example, suppose a sender wants to transmit five packets to the receiver. The sender sets the window size to three packets, which means it can send three packets before waiting for an acknowledgment from the receiver. The sender sends the first three packets, and the receiver acknowledges them. The sender then moves the window to the next three packets and sends them. The receiver acknowledges them as well, and the sender has successfully transmitted all five packets.

Flow Control Mechanisms

Flow control mechanisms ensure that data transmission occurs at a rate that the receiver can handle without overwhelming it. They prevent packet loss and unnecessary transmissions by regulating the amount of data that the sender can transmit at any given time.

There are two main flow control mechanisms:

Buffering: The receiver reserves a buffer space for incoming packets. The sender is allowed to transmit packets as long as there is enough space in the buffer. If the buffer reaches capacity, the receiver sends a signal to the sender to stop transmitting.

Window-based flow control: This mechanism is similar to the sliding window protocol. The receiver specifies the maximum number of packets that it can receive at any given time. The sender then sends packets up to the specified limit, and the receiver acknowledges them. The sender can only send packets after receiving an acknowledgment for the previously transmitted packets.

For example, suppose a sender wants to transmit ten packets to the receiver. The receiver specifies a window size of three. The sender sends the first three packets, and the receiver acknowledges them. The sender then sends the next three packets, and the receiver acknowledges them too. However, the receiver can only receive one more packet because its buffer is full. The sender waits for an acknowledgment before sending the next packet.

In conclusion, the sliding window protocol and flow control mechanisms are crucial for efficient and reliable data transmission in networking. They regulate the rate of data transmission and ensure that data is transmitted without loss or duplication. These mechanisms improve the overall performance of the network and enhance the end-user experience.

3.3   What are the differences between static and dynamic routing, and when would you use each?

Routing is the process of selecting the optimal path for data to travel from one network device to another. There are two main methods of routing: static and dynamic.

Static routing is a manual process where an administrator manually configures the routing table on each network device. Each route is entered into the table with a destination address and the exit interface or next-hop address to reach that destination. Once configured, the network device will always use that specific route until it is manually changed.

Dynamic routing, on the other hand, is an automatic process where a routing protocol is used to exchange information between network devices about available routes. The routing protocol will analyze the information, calculate the best path, and update the routing table accordingly. This type of routing is used in larger networks where the number of possible routes is large and changes frequently.

There are several advantages and disadvantages to each type of routing.

Static routing is relatively simple to configure and has low overhead, but it can be difficult to manage in larger networks since routes need to be manually configured on every network device. It also cannot adapt to changes in the network, such as device or link failures, without manual intervention. Static routing is generally best used in smaller networks with a limited number of routes that do not change frequently, such as in a small office or home network.

Dynamic routing, on the other hand, is more complex to configure and has higher overhead due to the routing protocol, but it can adapt to changes in the network automatically, making it ideal for large networks with a high number of routes that change frequently. Dynamic routing protocols can also support load balancing across multiple paths, providing redundancy in case of device or link failures, and can support advanced features such as route summarization, filtering and redistribution.

For example, in a small office network with only a few devices, static routing may be the best option since there are few routes and they are unlikely to change frequently. However, in a large enterprise network with multiple sites, hundreds of devices and multiple paths to reach different destinations, dynamic routing protocols such as OSPF or BGP would be a better choice since it can adapt to changes automatically, providing optimal paths to reach destinations reducing administrate overhead.

3.4 What is the purpose of the Address Resolution Protocol (ARP), and how does it work?

The Address Resolution Protocol (ARP) is a protocol used in computer networking to map a physical (MAC) address to an IP address. It is used to resolve the IP address of a device on a local network when only its physical address is known. This is necessary because the devices in a network communicate using physical addresses, while higher-level protocols (such as IP) use logical (IP) addresses.

ARP works by broadcasting a request message, known as an ARP request, to all nodes on the local network. The message contains the IP address for which the physical address is needed. The device whose IP address matches the address in the request responds with an ARP reply message, which contains its physical address. The requesting device stores the physical address in its ARP table, so that it can be used for future communication with that device.

For example, if a computer wants to send data to another device on the same network, it checks its ARP table to see if it already has the physical address for that device. If it does not, it sends an ARP request to obtain the address. Once it has the physical address, it can then communicate with the other device using that address.

ARP is a critical component of local area networks, as it allows devices to communicate with each other using physical addresses. Without ARP, network communication would be much more difficult and inefficient, as devices would have to rely on manual mapping of IP addresses to physical addresses.

3.5   Can you describe the basic process of the three-way handshake in TCP connections?

Sure! The three-way handshake is the process used by TCP (Transmission Control Protocol) to establish a connection between two hosts. It's called a "three-way" handshake because it involves three messages exchanged between the two hosts. The basic process of the three-way handshake is as follows:

1. SYN: The initiating host sends a SYN (synchronize) message to the other host. This message includes a randomly generated sequence number that is used to keep track of which messages have been sent and received.

2. SYN-ACK: The receiving host responds with a SYN-ACK (synchronize-acknowledge) message. This message includes its own randomly generated sequence number, as well as an acknowledgement number that is one greater than the initiating host's sequence number. This ac-

knowledges receipt of the SYN message and initializes the connection.

3. ACK: The initiating host responds with an ACK (acknowledge) message. This message includes the acknowledgement number that the receiving host sent in the SYN-ACK message. This acknowledges receipt of the SYN-ACK message and completes the three-way handshake.

Once the three-way handshake is complete, TCP has established a reliable connection between the two hosts. Both hosts can now start sending data to each other, and TCP guarantees that the data will be delivered in the correct order and without errors.

Here is an example of the three-way handshake in action:

1. The initiating host (let's call it Host A) sends a SYN message to the receiving host (Host B). The sequence number in the SYN message is, say, 100.

2. Host B responds with a SYN-ACK message. The sequence number in the SYN-ACK message is, say, 200 (randomly generated by Host B), and the acknowledgement number is 101 (Host A's sequence number plus one).

3. Host A responds with an ACK message. The acknowledgement number in the ACK message is 201 (Host B's sequence number plus one).

At this point, the three-way handshake is complete, and Host A and Host B can start sending data to each other over the TCP connection.

3.6   What is the role of the ICMP protocol, and how does it support IP networks?

The Internet Control Message Protocol (ICMP) is a network layer protocol that is used to report error conditions and provide diagnostic information for IP (Internet Protocol) networks. The ICMP protocol is a vital part of the networking protocol stack, providing essential feedback to network devices and helping to ensure that network traffic is flowing correctly.

One of the most important roles of the ICMP protocol is to provide feedback about packet delivery and routing. For example, when a packet is sent from one device to another, the ICMP protocol is used to send an "echo request" that asks the receiving device to return an "echo reply" to confirm that the packet was received correctly. If the receiving device does not respond, or if the packet is lost in transit, the ICMP protocol can be used to report the error back to the sender.

ICMP is also used to support other network functions, such as traceroute and ping, which are used to test network connectivity and measure packet delivery times. For example, the ping command uses ICMP echo requests and replies to test connectivity between two devices, while the traceroute command uses ICMP "time exceeded" messages to determine the path that packets take through a network.

In addition to packet delivery and diagnostic functions, the ICMP protocol can also be used for network management and control purposes. For example, routers often send ICMP redirect messages to inform hosts that a better route is available for a particular destination address.

Overall, the ICMP protocol is an essential component of IP networks, providing critical feedback and diagnostic information to ensure that network traffic is flowing smoothly and efficiently.

3.7   Can you explain the concept of port forwarding, and why it's used in some networking scenarios?

Port forwarding is a technique used in computer networking to allow external devices to access a specific resource or service on a local network. It involves redirecting traffic from a specified port on the router to a specific device on the network.

In most network setups, devices on the local network are assigned private IP addresses, while the router is given a public IP address by the internet service provider. When external devices try to access a resource on the local network, they send requests to the public IP address of the router. Without port forwarding, the router would simply discard these requests, as it wouldn't know which device on the local network the traffic is intended for.

Port forwarding solves this problem by allowing traffic from a specified port on the router to be redirected to a specific device on the network. For example, if you have a web server running on a device on your local network and want to make it accessible from the internet, you can set up port forwarding so that requests to port 80 (the default port for HTTP) on the router are forwarded to the web server on the local network.

Port forwarding is commonly used for a variety of scenarios, including:

1. Hosting services: If you want to host a server for a game, a website or any other service, you need to open specific ports for that service. If you use port forwarding you can allow external users to connect to that service on your local network.

2. Remote access: If you want to access resources on your local network, such as a file server or remote desktop, from an external location, you can use port forwarding to make the resources accessible over the internet.

3. Improved security: Port forwarding can increase security by restricting external access to only specific services or devices on the local network. By forwarding only the ports required for a specific service, you can reduce the risk of unauthorized access to your network.

Overall, port forwarding is a useful technique for allowing external devices to access resources on a local network. However, it does require careful configuration to ensure that only the necessary ports are opened and that security is maintained.

3.8   What are Quality of Service (QoS) mechanisms, and how do they help manage network resources?

Quality of Service (QoS) mechanisms are techniques used in computer networking to manage network resources effectively, ensuring that high-priority traffic receives preferential treatment over low-priority traffic. QoS enables network administrators to establish policies and controls to ensure that critical traffic receives the necessary bandwidth, low latency, and minimal packet loss, while also controlling and limiting traffic that is not as critical.

There are several types of QoS mechanisms, including:

1. Traffic Prioritization: Prioritizes network traffic based on defined rulesets. It allows network administrators to allocate network resources based on policies that define the criticality of different types of traffic. For example, video conferencing and voice-over-IP (VoIP) traffic require low latency, and consistent high-speed connectivity, while web browsing traffic may have relaxed requirements. The prioritization mechanism sorts packets into different queues based on the level of importance, and then allocates network resources accordingly.

2. Traffic Shaping: Traffic shaping controls traffic flow rate by regulating the amount of data sent and received at any given time. It can help prevent network congestion by limiting the amount of data that flows onto the network to ensure a smooth network operation. Traffic shaping can also reduce network jitter and ensure that critical traffic receives the appropriate level of resources.

3. Congestion Control: Congestion control aims to prevent network congestion by controlling the congestion window size, an algorithm that regulates the number of packets allowed on the network at any given time. Congestion control aims to balance the utilization of network resources by controlling the amount of data that is allowed to be transmitted across the network. Congestion Control Techniques, such as TCP and ATM (Asynchronous Transfer Mode), help in this respect by ensuring that traffic does not overwhelm the network capacity.

4. Packet Scheduling: Packet scheduling prioritizes the delivery of

packets based on several factors, including their priority level, source, and destination addresses. It helps reduce packet transmission delay and packet loss, ensuring that critical traffic is delivered reliably and consistently.

In conclusion, by using QoS mechanisms, network administrators can set priorities for different types of traffic, allocate network resources based on those priorities, and manage network traffic more effectively. This results in better network performance, reduced congestion, and increased reliability of mission-critical applications.

3.9   What is the difference between a stateful and stateless firewall?

A firewall is a security device which protects computers and networks from unauthorized access by filtering incoming and outgoing traffic. There are two types of firewalls: stateful and stateless.

A stateless firewall, also known as a packet filter, examines each packet of data that passes through it and makes decisions based on information it finds in the packet header, such as the source and destination addresses, ports and protocol types. It works by comparing the packets to a set of predefined rules, and if a packet matches one of these rules, it is either allowed or denied. Stateless firewalls do not maintain any information about previous traffic, so they cannot determine whether a packet belongs to an existing session or not. For example, a stateless firewall might allow all traffic on port 80 (the port used for HTTP traffic), regardless of whether the traffic is part of an existing HTTP session or not. This lack of context can make stateless firewalls less effective at preventing certain types of attacks, such as denial-of-service attacks or attacks that exploit protocol vulnerabilities.

On the other hand, a stateful firewall, also known as a dynamic packet filter, not only filters traffic based on header information, but also keeps track of the state of connections passing through it. Stateful firewalls examine the entire packet, including the payload, and are able to determine whether a packet belongs to an existing session or not. They maintain information about the state of connections (such as IP addresses, port numbers and sequence numbers), and use this information to make more intelligent filtering decisions. For example, a stateful firewall might be configured to allow incoming traffic only if it is part of an established and authorized session, and to monitor the session's state to ensure that it remains valid. This makes stateful firewalls more effective at preventing certain types of attacks, as they are able to filter out potentially malicious connection attempts that use invalid or unauthorized session information.

In general, stateful firewalls provide more comprehensive protection than stateless firewalls, although they are more resource-intensive and some performance issues may arise. For this reason, stateful firewalls are typically used in environments that require higher levels of security, while stateless firewalls are used in simpler, less complex network architectures.

3.10   Can you explain the role of network monitoring tools, and name some common ones used in the industry?

Network monitoring tools are an essential part of managing and maintaining a computer network. They allow network administrators to monitor the performance and security of the network, as well as identify and troubleshoot problems in real-time. The role of network monitoring tools is to provide visibility into the network, gather data and provide alerts when unusual or problematic behavior is detected.

There are several types of network monitoring tools, including:

1. Network Performance Monitoring (NPM) tools: These tools monitor the network traffic, bandwidth utilization, and performance metrics of different devices such as routers, switches, servers, and applications.

2. Network Security Monitoring (NSM) tools: These tools monitor the network for security threats, including malware, viruses, intrusion attempts, and other suspicious behavior.

3. Packet Analyzers: These tools capture, analyze, and decode net-

work packets to help administrators diagnose network-related problems.

Some common network monitoring tools used in the industry are:

1. Cisco Prime: A comprehensive network monitoring tool that offers network device detection and topology, automated device configuration, and enhanced security features.

2. SolarWinds Network Performance Monitor (NPM): Provides in-depth performance metrics for routers, switches, and other network devices, helps diagnose issues and offers automatic remediation options.

3. Nagios: An open-source solution for monitoring network, systems and applications availability, and performance.

4. Wireshark: A packet analyzer tool that can capture, analyze and troubleshoot network traffic.

5. PRTG Network Monitor: A comprehensive network management tool that includes network performance monitoring, bandwidth monitoring, and network traffic analysis.

In conclusion, network monitoring tools are essential to ensuring the proper functioning and optimal performance of computer networks. By monitoring critical performance and security metrics, network monitoring tools provide network administrators the information they need to quickly diagnose and resolve issues that could otherwise negatively affect the network and the services it provides.

3.11   What is the Spanning Tree Protocol (STP), and why is it important for preventing network loops?

The Spanning Tree Protocol (STP) is a networking protocol used to prevent loops in a network with redundant paths. The protocol constructs a spanning tree, a logical tree-like structure, by selectively disabling redundant links that would otherwise create loops.

In a network with redundant paths, packets may be forwarded along multiple paths, leading to loops. These loops can significantly degrade network performance and ultimately lead to a network outage. The STP algorithm prevents loops by continuously monitoring the network for redundant links and disabling them as necessary. The algorithm elects a root bridge, which becomes the central point of the spanning tree, and then disables all the links that are not on the shortest path between a network device and the root bridge.

To achieve this, each bridge or switch participating in the STP exchanges Bridge Protocol Data Units (BPDUs), containing information such as the bridge ID, interface cost, and the root bridge ID. The switches use this information to determine the root bridge and the shortest path to it, and also to monitor the status of other switches and links in the network.

In summary, the STP is essential for preventing network loops and ensuring network reliability. By carefully disabling redundant links that would otherwise create loops, the STP algorithm creates a logical tree-like structure, which provides a loop-free path for packet forwarding. This ensures that network traffic reaches its destination without getting caught in an endless loop, thereby improving network performance and reliability.

3.12   How does traceroute work, and what is its purpose in network troubleshooting?

Traceroute is a network diagnostic tool that shows the path taken by packets between a source host and a destination host in the Internet. It works by sending packets with gradually increasing Time-to-Live (TTL) values and noting the address of the router that discards each packet because it exceeded its TTL value.

When a packet is sent from the source host, it is given a TTL value of 1. The first router it encounters decrements the TTL value by 1 and discards the packet when the TTL value becomes 0. The router then sends an ICMP "time exceeded" message back to the source host, which includes the IP address of the router. Traceroute displays this information to the user, and then sends another packet with a TTL value of 2, and repeats the same process. This continues until the packet finally reaches the destination host, or until a maximum number of hops has been reached, which is usually set at 30.

The purpose of traceroute is to enable network administrators and users to identify the path packets take between two hosts in the Internet, and to diagnose problems with network connectivity. Traceroute can be used to identify the IP addresses of routers along the path, which can help in troubleshooting connectivity issues such as packet loss, high latency or path asymmetry. It also allows for the detection of routing loops or black holes, where packets may be discarded without any notification to the sender. By using traceroute, network administrators can quickly pinpoint the location of a problem on a network, and take appropriate actions to resolve it.

For example, suppose a user is experiencing slow Internet speeds when trying to access a website. By running traceroute to the website's IP address, the user can identify if there are any routers causing delay along the path, and if so, which ones. This information can help the user or network administrator to identify the specific network issue and take corrective measures.

3.13 Can you describe the difference between symmetric and asymmetric encryption, and provide examples of each?

Encryption is the process of converting plaintext data into a ciphertext format that is unreadable for unauthorized users. Encryption techniques can be divided into two categories: symmetric and asymmetric encryption.

Symmetric encryption (also known as shared-secret encryption) uses the same secret key for both encryption and decryption processes. The sender and the receiver must have the same key in order to communicate. A commonly used symmetric encryption algorithm is Advanced Encryption Standard (AES).

As an example, let us consider a scenario where Alice wants to send a message to Bob using symmetric encryption. Alice encrypts the message using a secret key and sends the ciphertext to Bob. Bob then decrypts the ciphertext using the same secret key and retrieves the original plaintext message.

Asymmetric encryption (also known as public-key encryption) uses a pair of keys for encryption and decryption, unlike symmetric encryption which uses just one key. The two keys are mathematically related, but one key is kept private and the other is made public. The public key can be shared with anyone, whereas the private key must be kept secret. RSA encryption is a popular example of asymmetric encryption.

As an example, let us consider a scenario where Alice wants to send a message to Bob using asymmetric encryption. Bob generates a pair of keys (a private key and a public key) and shares the public key with Alice. Alice encrypts the message using Bob's public key and sends the ciphertext to Bob. Bob then decrypts the message using his private key and retrieves the original plaintext message.

In summary, symmetric encryption uses the same secret key for both encryption and decryption, while asymmetric encryption uses a pair of keys (a public key and a private key) for encryption and decryption. Symmetric encryption is faster than asymmetric encryption but has security issues because of the need to share the secret key. Asymmetric encryption provides better security but is slower than symmetric encryption.

In practice, both encryption types are used in different scenarios. Symmetric encryption is commonly used in scenarios where speed and efficiency are crucial, such as encrypted messaging. Asymmetric encryption is commonly used in scenarios where a high level of security is required, such as securing online transactions or securing the transmission of sensitive data.

3.14 What is a proxy server, and how can it be used to improve network security and performance?

A proxy server is an intermediary server that sits between a client and a server. When a client requests a resource or service from a server, the client sends the request to the proxy server, which then forwards the request to the destination server on behalf of the client.

Proxy servers can be used to improve network security in a number of ways. One of the primary benefits of using a proxy server is that it can act as a buffer between a user's device and the internet, which can help to prevent direct attacks on the user's device. By intercepting and screening traffic, a proxy server can filter out potentially harmful traffic, such as malware, viruses, spam, and phishing attempts, before it reaches the user's device. This not only helps to improve security, but also enhances performance, since the user's device is not bogged down by unwanted traffic.

Another way in which proxy servers can enhance network security is by providing anonymity for users. By using a proxy server, users can mask their IP address and location, which can help to protect their privacy and prevent tracking by hackers, advertisers, and other third parties.

In addition to improving network security, proxy servers can also be used to enhance network performance. By caching frequently requested content, such as web pages and images, a proxy server can reduce the amount of bandwidth needed to transmit data between the client and server. This not only speeds up network performance for users, but also reduces costs for businesses that need to purchase additional bandwidth to handle high traffic volumes.

Overall, proxy servers offer a wide range of benefits for both security and performance. By acting as a buffer between clients and servers, proxy servers can protect devices from direct attacks and unwanted traffic, provide anonymity for users, and help to speed up network performance by caching frequently requested content.

3.15   How do Content Delivery Networks (CDNs) work, and what are their advantages?

Content Delivery Networks (CDNs) are used to deliver content, such as text, images, video, and other media, to users quickly and efficiently. They work by distributing the content across a network of servers located in different geographic locations, closer to where the users are accessing the content from.

When a user requests content, the CDN system automatically selects the server closest to the user, which speeds up the delivery of the content. The CDN can also prioritize the delivery of popular content, which reduces the load on any individual server and improves the overall performance of the system.

CDNs offer several advantages for website owners and users, including:

1. Improved website performance: By distributing content across multiple servers, CDNs can reduce the burden on any one server and improve the overall performance of the website. This results in faster load times for users, which can lead to increased engagement and lower bounce rates.

2. Increased reliability: With multiple servers available, if one server fails, the CDN can automatically route traffic to an available server. This means that users can access the website even if there are technical issues with the primary server.

3. Better security: CDNs can offer enhanced security features such as SSL/TLS encryption and DDoS protection, which can help protect against attacks that could slow down the website or compromise user data.

4. Cost savings: By using a CDN, website owners can reduce the cost of server maintenance and bandwidth usage. This is because the CDN provider handles the traffic management and content delivery, reducing the load on the website's own servers.

A good example of a CDN is Cloudflare, which offers a suite of services including content delivery, security, and performance optimization. By leveraging their extensive network of servers around the world, Cloudflare can deliver content quickly and securely, and help website owners improve their website performance and reliability.

In summary, CDNs offer a reliable and efficient way to deliver content to users around the world, with benefits including improved website performance, increased reliability, better security, and cost savings for website owners.

3.16 What is the difference between the iterative and recursive query process in DNS resolution?

DNS (Domain Name System) is a critical protocol used on the internet to resolve domain names into IP addresses. DNS resolution can be carried out through two methods- iterative and recursive resolution.

In recursive resolution, the DNS client sends a query to a DNS resolver, which then sends requests to other DNS servers until it gets a response. The resolver takes care of the entire process, and the client only receives the final result. Recursive resolution is typically used by end-user devices, such as laptops and smartphones, which do not have their own dedicated DNS servers.

On the other hand, iterative resolution requires the client to initiate the process by sending queries to DNS servers until it receives the final result. The client is responsible for the whole process, which involves querying each DNS server, analyzing the responses, and determining the next DNS server to query until it reaches the final resolution.

Here's an example to illustrate the difference between iterative and recursive resolution:

Suppose a client wants to resolve the domain name www.example.com. In recursive resolution, the client sends a query to the resolver, which starts the resolution process. The resolver can then send requests to various DNS servers, such as root servers, top-level domain (TLD) servers, and authoritative servers until it receives the final IP address.

The resolver then sends the IP address back to the client.

In iterative resolution, the client initiates the process by sending its query to a DNS server. If the queried DNS server is able to resolve the domain name, it responds with the IP address. If not, the server sends a referral response to the client, which contains the next DNS server to query. The client continues this process until it receives the final IP address.

In conclusion, iterative resolution requires more effort from the client in terms of querying and analyzing responses, whereas recursive resolution shifts that burden to the resolver. Both techniques have their strengths and weaknesses and are used in different scenarios depending on the requirements of the client and the characteristics of the DNS infrastructure.

3.17   Can you explain the concept of load balancing, and why it is important for network performance?

Load balancing refers to the process of distributing traffic across multiple servers or network resources to optimize resource utilization, increase availability, and enhance performance. Load balancing enables systems administrators to manage high volumes of network traffic, distribute resources efficiently, and reduce downtime.

Load balancing is important for network performance because it ensures that no single server or resource is responsible for handling all the network traffic, which can quickly overwhelm and cause the resource to fail. By sharing the network load across multiple resources, load balancing improves network scalability, reliability, and availability.

One common use case for load balancing is in web server clusters. When a web server receives a request for a webpage, it can use load balancing to distribute the request across a group of servers instead of handling it on a single server. This allows the web server cluster to handle more requests and respond more quickly to client requests, thereby increasing user satisfaction.

Load balancing can be performed using a variety of methods, such as round-robin, least connections, IP hash, and more. These methods each have their own advantages and disadvantages, depending on the specific requirements of the network environment.

In summary, load balancing is an essential concept in computer networking that enables organizations to optimize resource utilization, enhance performance, and ensure high levels of availability and reliability.

3.18 What is the purpose of the Simple Network Management Protocol (SNMP), and how is it used to manage network devices?

The Simple Network Management Protocol (SNMP) is a widely-used protocol for monitoring and managing network devices. Its primary purpose is to collect and organize information about network devices, and to allow network administrators to configure and control those devices remotely.

SNMP consists of a set of standards defined by the Internet Engineering Task Force (IETF), which specify the format and content of messages exchanged between network devices and management systems. SNMP management systems typically use a hierarchical structure known as the Management Information Base (MIB), which defines the structure and content of the data that can be accessed and manipulated by the protocol.

To use SNMP to manage a network device, a network administrator must typically configure the device to support SNMP, including setting up an SNMP agent that can communicate with SNMP management systems. The administrator can then use SNMP management software to connect to the device and access the data stored in its MIB. This data may include information about device configuration and performance, such as interface statistics, error logs, and other metrics.

SNMP management systems can also be used to configure and control network devices, such as by setting configuration parameters, resetting or restarting devices, or triggering alarms or other actions based on network events or performance thresholds.

Overall, SNMP is a powerful tool for monitoring and managing network devices, and provides a flexible and standardized way for network administrators to monitor and control complex networks with many interconnected components.

3.19   What are the differences between routing protocols like OSPF, EIGRP, and BGP?

Routing protocols are used by routers to dynamically share information about the network and to determine the best path for data to travel from one network to another. There are several different routing protocols, including OSPF, EIGRP, and BGP. Here are the differences between these three protocols:

1. OSPF (Open Shortest Path First) is a link-state protocol. It calculates the shortest path to a destination by considering the cost of each link in the network. OSPF routers create a map of the network and use this map to determine the best route for data to travel. OSPF is typically used within an organization or a single autonomous system.

2. EIGRP (Enhanced Interior Gateway Routing Protocol) is a distance-vector protocol that was developed by Cisco. It takes into account both the bandwidth and delay of a link to determine the best route for data to travel. EIGRP is faster than OSPF at converging and adjusting to changes in the network, making it suitable for large and complex networks.

3. BGP (Border Gateway Protocol) is a path-vector protocol that is used to exchange routing information between different autonomous systems (ASes) on the Internet. BGP determines the best path for data to travel based on policies set by network administrators. BGP is slower to converge than OSPF and EIGRP, but is necessary for

large-scale Internet routing.

In summary, OSPF is used within a single organization or autonomous system, EIGRP is used for large and complex networks, and BGP is used for interconnecting different autonomous systems on the Internet. Each protocol has its strengths and weaknesses, and network administrators must choose the appropriate protocol based on the needs of their network.

3.20   Can you describe the concept of network segmentation, and why it is important for security and performance?

Network segmentation is the process of dividing a larger network into smaller, separate subnetworks, each with its own unique characteristics, security policy, and access control. This is done by creating virtual or physical barriers between the different network zones or segments, which can be based on a variety of criteria such as IP addresses, applications, user groups, or devices.

Network segmentation is important for both security and performance reasons. In terms of security, it helps to limit the scope of a potential attack by containing it within a smaller segment of the network. For example, a compromised device in one segment will not be able to access resources in another segment unless explicitly granted access. This reduces the risk of lateral movement and limits the potential damage that an attacker can cause.

In addition, network segmentation can simplify security policy management and reduce the attack surface by reducing the number of devices and services visible to the outside world. This is particularly important for organizations that handle sensitive data, such as financial or healthcare institutions, where compliance with regulatory requirements and data privacy laws is crucial. By segmenting the network and applying strict access controls, these organizations can mitigate the risk of data breaches and cyber attacks.

From a performance perspective, network segmentation can also help to improve network efficiency and availability by reducing congestion and isolating faulty or poorly performing segments. For example, if a portion of the network experiences high traffic or other performance issues, the impact will be limited to that segment and not affect the rest of the network. This can help to minimize downtime and ensure that critical business applications remain accessible and responsive.

Overall, network segmentation is a critical aspect of network design and security that can help organizations to improve their security posture, simplify management, and enhance network performance.

Chapter 4

Advanced

4.1 Can you explain the differences between various types of VPNs, such as site-to-site, remote access, and SSL VPNs?

Virtual Private Networks (VPN) are secure private connections over the internet that allow remote access to a private network or its resources. There are several types of VPNs, each with its own unique features and intended use cases.

- Site-to-Site VPN: Site-to-Site VPN, also known as router-to-router VPN, connects two or more sites of an organization or different organizations with a secure connection over the internet. The communication between the sites is encrypted and secure. Site-to-Site VPNs are commonly used to connect branch offices, data centers, and remote offices of a company, enabling employees to access resources in the central or main location. In a Site-to-Site VPN, the corporate LAN or WAN is extended to the remote sites, and routing is carried out between the sites.

- Remote Access VPN: A Remote Access VPN, also called a Client-to-Site VPN, or a Virtual Private Dial-up Network (VPDN), allows remote employees or clients to securely connect to the organization's network over the internet. A Remote Access VPN is more like an on-demand service for the clients to connect to the corporate network from any remote location using a software client installed on their computer or mobile device. When the connection is established, the client computer appears as if it is directly connected to the corporate network. The Remote Access VPN uses client authentication, tunneling protocols, and encryption to ensure security and privacy.

- SSL VPN: An SSL VPN creates a secure connection between a client and a server over the internet using the HTTPS protocol. Unlike traditional VPNs, which require a VPN client to be installed on the user's device, SSL VPNs do not require any additional software to be installed, making them easier to use. SSL VPNs are mostly used to provide secure access for remote users to web applications and services. The web application acts as the endpoint for the SSL VPN service, and the user can access it through a standard web browser. SSL VPNs use SSL/TLS encryption to secure the communication between the client and server.

In summary, Site-to-Site VPNs connect two or more sites; Remote Access VPNs connect remote users to the internal company network, and SSL VPNs connect remote users to web applications and services. Each type of VPN has its own unique features and use cases, and it's essential to understand the differences between them to choose the right VPN for your organization's needs.

4.2   How does Multiprotocol Label Switching (MPLS) work, and what are its advantages in network performance and management?

Multiprotocol Label Switching (MPLS) is a mechanism used in computer networking that enables the efficient and high-speed transfer of data packets over a network. It works by labeling data packets with unique identifiers, known as labels, allowing routers to quickly and reliably direct the packets through the network.

When a packet enters the network, the first router along its path assigns a label to it. Each subsequent router along the path prepends additional labels to the packet, indicating the path it should follow through the network. When the packet reaches its destination, the final router removes the labels and forwards the packet to its intended recipient.

One of the advantages of MPLS is that it enables traffic engineering. By manipulating the labels assigned to packets, traffic can be routed through specific paths in the network, allowing for better utilization of network resources and more efficient data transfer. For example, traffic that requires low latency can be prioritized and routed through a path that ensures faster transmission, while traffic that can tolerate high latency can be routed through a separate path to maximize overall network utilization.

MPLS also offers improved Quality of Service (QoS) capabilities, allowing network administrators to classify and prioritize different types of traffic. By assigning labels to packets based on their content, such as voice or video data, QoS policies can be applied to ensure that high-priority traffic is given preferential treatment over lower-priority traffic.

Another advantage of MPLS is its scalability. As networks grow more complex and data volumes increase, MPLS can handle the increased traffic without sacrificing performance. Traditional IP routing protocols may experience delays or bottlenecks under increased load, but MPLS can handle large volumes of traffic with ease.

Overall, MPLS offers a number of advantages over traditional IP routing protocols. It enables traffic engineering and QoS functionalities, improves scalability, and offers more efficient utilization of network resources. These advantages make MPLS a popular choice for enterprise networks and service providers who require fast, reliable data transfer with minimal delays.

4.3   What is the role of network virtualization, and how do technologies like SDN and NFV fit into it?

Network virtualization is the process of abstracting the physical network resources such as servers, routers, switches, etc. to create a logically isolated network. The primary objective is to provide a virtual environment that is independent of the underlying physical infrastructure without any interference from other tenants or applications on the same network.

The concept of network virtualization allows users to deploy multiple virtual networks on top of a single physical infrastructure, each with its own unique attributes such as IP addressing, subnetting, routing, security policies, and protocols. This virtualization of the network infrastructure helps improve resilience, flexibility, scalability, and security while reducing operational costs.

Software-defined networking (SDN) and network function virtualization (NFV) are two core technologies that support network virtualization.

SDN is an approach to network design that abstracts the control plane, which decides how traffic is forwarded, from the data plane, which is responsible for moving traffic. This separation allows operators to manage and configure the network centrally, making it easier to deploy and manage services. With SDN, network architectures are programmable and centralized, enabling administrators to automate or reconfigure network functions in real-time using open APIs, which significantly reduce network complexity and operational costs.

NFV, on the other hand, is a technique for replacing dedicated hardware-based network functions with virtualized software applications that can run on standard servers or cloud infrastructure. The aim is to run network functions such as firewalls, routers, load balancers, and intrusion detection systems, in software to make network management more agile, scalable, and cost-effective. Using NFV, virtualized network functions (VNFs) can be deployed dynamically, moved between servers, or scaled up or down based on demand, just like any other software application running on servers or cloud infrastructure.

In conclusion, network virtualization is an essential concept that improves network performance and simplifies management while reducing operational costs. Technologies such as SDN and NFV help to implement network virtualization by providing virtualized software and centralized management that enhance network agility, scalability, and security.

4.4 Can you explain the various tunneling protocols, such as GRE, L2TP, and IPsec, and their use cases?

Tunneling protocols are used to encapsulate one network protocol inside another network protocol, allowing data to be sent securely over an unsecured network. There are several tunneling protocols available, including GRE, L2TP, and IPsec.

GRE (Generic Routing Encapsulation):

GRE is a simple and lightweight tunneling protocol that is used to encapsulate one protocol inside another protocol. GRE is often used with IPsec for creating VPNs that carry multiple protocols. GRE encapsulates packets by adding a header that includes information about the original packet's source and destination.

GRE is commonly used in situations where a network administrator wants to connect two networks that use different protocols. For example, a network administrator might use GRE to connect an IPv4 network to an IPv6 network.

L2TP (Layer 2 Tunneling Protocol):

L2TP is a tunneling protocol that is used to support virtual private networks (VPNs). L2TP is often used with IPsec for securing the VPN connection. L2TP encapsulates the original packet inside an L2TP packet, which is then sent over the internet.

L2TP is commonly used in situations where a network administrator wants to connect remote users to a local network. L2TP can provide remote access to resources, such as printers, file servers, and other resources located on the local network.

IPsec (Internet Protocol Security):

IPsec is a set of protocols that is used to provide security for internet protocol (IP) networks. IPsec can be used to create secure tunnels for VPNs or for securing direct connections between two hosts.

IPsec uses two main protocols: Authentication Header (AH) and Encapsulating Security Payload (ESP). AH provides authentication and integrity checking for IP packets, while ESP provides encryption and confidentiality for IP packets.

IPsec is commonly used in situations where a network administrator wants to secure data sent over an unsecured network. IPsec provides a strong level of security and can be used to protect sensitive data, such as financial information or corporate secrets.

In summary, tunneling protocols such as GRE, L2TP, and IPsec are used to encapsulate one protocol inside another protocol to provide security and privacy when transmitting data over the internet. GRE is used when connecting two networks that use different protocols, L2TP is used for remote access to local resources, and IPsec is used for securing data sent over an unsecured network.

4.5   How do the different types of intrusion detection and prevention systems (IDS/IPS) work, and when should they be used?

Intrusion Detection and Prevention Systems (IDS/IPS) are critical components of any organization's cybersecurity posture. These systems work to detect and prevent unauthorized access to computer networks and systems.

IDS and IPS are two types of systems that work together to protect against cyber attacks. IDS systems work by monitoring network traffic and looking for suspicious activity that might indicate a cyber attack. These systems can be configured to look for specific types of traffic or activity, such as port scanning, malware infections, or attempts to exploit known vulnerabilities.

IPS systems are more proactive and work to prevent attacks from occurring. These systems use techniques such as packet filtering, signature-based detection, and behavior-based detection to prevent malicious traffic from entering the network.

There are several types of IDS and IPS systems, each with its own strengths and weaknesses. Some common types of IDS systems include:

1. Network-based IDS (NIDS): These systems monitor network traffic to identify potential attacks. NIDS systems can be an effective way to detect attacks that target specific network protocols or processes.

2. Host-based IDS (HIDS): These systems monitor activity on individual hosts, such as servers or workstations. HIDS systems are useful for identifying attacks on specific machines.

3. Anomaly-based IDS: These systems look for unusual behavior that might indicate an attack, such as unusual network traffic or unusual system resource usage.

4. Signature-based IDS: These systems use pre-defined signatures to detect known attacks. Signature-based systems can be useful for detecting common types of attacks, but they can be less effective against new or unknown attacks.

There are also several types of IPS systems that work to prevent attacks from occurring. These include:

1. Packet filtering: This is the simplest form of IPS and involves blocking traffic based on pre-defined rules. Packet filtering can be effective at blocking known threats, but it can be less effective against more sophisticated attacks.

2. Signature-based IPS: These systems use pre-defined signatures to block known threats. Signature-based IPS systems can be effective at blocking common types of attacks, but they can be less effective against new or unknown threats.

3. Behavior-based IPS: These systems use machine learning and other

techniques to identify unusual behavior that might indicate an attack. Behavior-based IPS systems can be effective at detecting new and unknown threats, but they can also be prone to false positives.

In general, organizations should use a combination of IDS and IPS systems to provide comprehensive protection against cyber attacks. IDS systems are useful for detecting attacks that might already be occurring, while IPS systems work to prevent attacks from occurring in the first place. However, organizations should also be aware of the limitations of these systems and should supplement them with other security measures, such as firewalls, secure coding practices, and user education.

4.6   What is the role of a Network Time Protocol (NTP) server, and why is time synchronization important in networking?

A Network Time Protocol (NTP) server is responsible for providing accurate time information to network devices. It does this by synchronizing its own clock with one or more reference clocks from a trusted time source, such as a GPS receiver or atomic clock. Network devices then query the NTP server to obtain accurate time information, which is critical for proper network operation.

Time synchronization is important in networking for several reasons. Firstly, accurate time is essential for effective network communication. This is because network protocols rely on synchronized clocks to coordinate the transmission and receipt of data packets. If clocks are not synchronized, packets may be delayed or lost, leading to degraded network performance.

Secondly, time synchronization is crucial for security. Many security mechanisms, such as digital certificates and Kerberos authentication, rely on accurate time to ensure that network transactions occur in the correct order and are not vulnerable to replay attacks. Without synchronized clocks, attackers could potentially intercept and replay network traffic to gain unauthorized access to systems or data.

Finally, time synchronization is important for compliance with regulatory requirements. Many industries, such as finance and healthcare, are required to maintain accurate records of network activity for auditing and legal purposes. Synchronized clocks are essential for ensuring the accuracy and integrity of these records.

In summary, the role of an NTP server is to provide accurate time information to network devices, which is crucial for effective network communication, security, and regulatory compliance.

4.7   Can you explain the concept of route summarization, and why it is important for routing efficiency?

Route summarization, also known as route aggregation, is a technique used in computer networking to reduce the size of the routing table by consolidating multiple smaller network prefixes into a single, larger prefix. This is accomplished by creating a more general, summarized route that encapsulates the smaller, more specific routes.

For example, suppose a network has the following five subnets: 10.1.1.0/24, 10.1.2.0/24, 10.1.3.0/24, 10.1.4.0/24, and 10.1.5.0/24. These subnets can be summarized into a single prefix of 10.1.0.0/16. This means that any traffic destined for any of the five subnets will be routed to the 10.1.0.0/16 network and then forwarded to the appropriate subnet based on its individual subnet mask.

One of the main advantages of route summarization is that it reduces the size of the routing table. In large networks, the routing table can become unwieldy, containing hundreds or even thousands of entries. This can lead to performance problems such as slow routing updates, high memory usage, and increased CPU load. By summarizing routes, the routing table size can be greatly reduced, resulting in more efficient routing updates and reduced memory and CPU usage.

Another advantage is that route summarization can also help to reduce the number of routing protocol updates that are needed across the network. This is because routing protocols typically only advertise summarized routes rather than individual subnets. This reduces the amount of unnecessary traffic on the network and helps to improve overall network performance.

In addition, route summarization can help to improve the security of the network by hiding the internal network structure. By summarizing routes, it becomes more difficult for potential attackers to determine the exact network topology and identify potential targets.

Overall, route summarization is an important technique for managing and optimizing large networks. It helps to reduce the size of routing tables, improve routing performance, and enhance network security.

4.8   How does Border Gateway Protocol (BGP) path selection work, and what factors influence the decision-making process?

Border Gateway Protocol (BGP) is a routing protocol used in the Internet to exchange routing information between different Autonomous Systems (AS). BGP is based on the path-vector protocol which allows a router to make routing decisions based on the complete path of an IP packet, rather than simply the next-hop router.

BGP path selection is based on a set of rules, which are commonly referred to as the BGP decision-making process. The BGP decision-making process uses a combination of factors to select the best path to a specific destination network. The following are the factors that influence the BGP path selection process:

1. Highest Local Preference: The Local Preference (LP) is used to indicate the preferred path for incoming traffic within an Autonomous System (AS). A BGP router selects the path with the highest Local Preference value as the preferred route. For example, if an AS has two connections with different Local Preference values, BGP selects the path with the higher Local Preference value.

2. Shortest AS Path: BGP also prefers the path with the shortest

Autonomous System path. This means that BGP routers will prefer a path that traverses the fewest number of ASes. For example, if an IP packet has two paths, one with three ASes and the other with five ASes, BGP will select the path with three ASes as the preferred route.

3. Origin Type: BGP also takes into account the type of the route's origin. For example, BGP prefers a route that has an origin in the local AS (e.g., originated by the local router) over a route that has an origin in a neighboring AS.

4. Multi-Exit Discriminator (MED): Sometimes referred to as the "metric," the MED is a value that is used by the local AS to indicate the preferred path for outgoing traffic. BGP selects the path with the lowest MED value as the preferred route. However, MED is only used when comparing routes from the same neighboring AS.

5. eBGP over iBGP: BGP prefers a route that is learned from an External BGP (eBGP) peer over a route learned from an Internal BGP (iBGP) peer. This is because eBGP routes provide better reachability than iBGP routes.

6. Lowest IP address: If all other factors are equal, BGP selects the path with the lowest router ID or IP address as the preferred route.

To illustrate the BGP decision-making process, consider a scenario where there are two paths for a specific destination network. Path 1 has a Local Preference of 200, an AS path length of three, and an origin type of eBGP. Path 2 has a Local Preference of 150, an AS path length of four, and an origin type of iBGP. In this scenario, BGP would select Path 1 as the preferred route because it has a higher Local Preference value, a shorter AS path, and was learned from an eBGP peer.

In conclusion, BGP path selection is a complex process that takes into consideration several factors that influence the routing decision. Understanding these factors can help network engineers optimize their network's routing policies and ensure that traffic is being routed efficiently.

4.9   What are the key considerations for implementing network redundancy and high availability?

Network redundancy and high availability are critical elements in ensuring that a network can sustain its operations with minimal to no downtime. There are several key considerations to keep in mind when implementing network redundancy and high availability.

1. Identify the critical components: Start by identifying the critical components of the network that need redundancy and high availability. This could include routers, switches, firewalls, servers, or storage devices. It is important to identify the critical components to determine where redundancy is needed and the level of availability required.

2. Redundant hardware: Implement redundant hardware for the critical components to ensure that there is no single point of failure. This can be accomplished through different methods such as using redundant power supplies or network interface cards, deploying redundant switches in a redundant topology, or configuring failover between redundant firewalls.

For example, the network can be designed with two core switches connected through two separate links, so that if one switch or link fails, the other one can automatically take over, providing automatic switch redundancy.

3. Redundant paths: Implement redundant paths to ensure that traffic can continue to flow in case of a network outage or failure. This can be achieved by using technologies such as link aggregation, Virtual Router Redundancy Protocol (VRRP) or Hot Standby Router Protocol (HSRP) for routing protocols.

For example, Link aggregation is a technique in which multiple physical links are bundled together to form a single logical link, increasing bandwidth and providing redundancy. VRRP and HSRP allow for two or more routers to work together to present the appearance of a single virtual router to the hosts on a LAN.

4. Network monitoring: Network monitoring is critical in identify-

ing network problems and failures. It is important to have real-time monitoring of the network devices to quickly detect and resolve issues.

For example, network monitoring software can be deployed to track key performance indicators of the network devices, such as CPU utilization, packet loss, and traffic volume.

5. Disaster recovery plan: A disaster recovery plan is important to ensure that the network can quickly recover from a catastrophic event. The plan should include the procedures to follow in case of a major outage, including the backup and restore of critical data and configurations.

In conclusion, implementing network redundancy and high availability can be achieved through redundant hardware, redundant paths, network monitoring, disaster recovery planning, and other measures. Ensuring that the network remains operational with minimal downtime requires a comprehensive approach to identifying critical components, designing redundancies where necessary, and implementing network monitoring and disaster recovery planning.

4.10 How does traffic shaping and policing work, and how do they help manage network congestion?

Traffic shaping and policing are techniques used in computer networking to manage network congestion. Traffic shaping is a technique used to control the rate at which data is transmitted over a network, while traffic policing is a technique used to monitor and enforce traffic rules and regulations on a network.

Traffic shaping manages bandwidth by delaying packets at the source, which smooths out the transmission of data over time. This technique is used when network traffic exceeds available bandwidth, and traffic shaping is necessary to prevent the network from becoming congested. The idea behind traffic shaping is to limit the sending rate of data on a particular link to avoid congestion.

Traffic shaping is accomplished through a variety of algorithms that aim to reduce congestion in the network, including token bucket and leaky bucket algorithms. These algorithms monitor the amount of traffic going through a particular network link and adjust the rate at which data is transmitted to ensure that the network does not become congested.

For example, consider a network with a maximum bandwidth of 100 Mbps, but the traffic flow exceeds 120 Mbps for a few minutes. If traffic shaping is not in place, this would lead to network congestion and packet loss. However, if traffic shaping is used, packets can be delayed at the source, so the bandwidth usage is smoothed out, and packets are delivered in a more controlled way resulting in reduced congestion and packet loss.

Traffic policing, on the other hand, enforces the rules and regulations on a network. It ensures that each user is not consuming more than their fair share of bandwidth, which can lead to congestion and slowdowns.

Generally, traffic policing provides a flexible way to shape the traffic based on an organization's specific needs. For example, an organization can prioritize different types of traffic depending on its importance, such as video conferencing and email. It also helps in enforcing policies like data usage limit or SLA commitments.

In conclusion, both traffic shaping and policing are essential techniques for managing network congestion. Traffic shaping helps in managing bandwidth by controlling the rate at which data is transmitted over a network, while traffic policing enforces rules and regulations on the network to ensure that each user is not exceeding their fair share of bandwidth. Together, they work to ensure that network bandwidth is utilized efficiently and effectively, reducing congestion and improving network performance.

4.11 What are the key differences between network access control (NAC) solutions, such as 802.1X and MAC filtering?

Network Access Control (NAC) solutions are used to identify and authenticate users and devices on a network before granting access to network resources.

802.1X and MAC filtering are two common types of NAC solutions. While both solutions achieve the same goal of providing secure access to network resources, they differ in their approach to network security.

802.1X is an authentication protocol that uses Extensible Authentication Protocol (EAP) to authenticate clients before they are allowed access to the network. With 802.1X, clients must provide valid credentials, such as a username and password, or a digital certificate, to be granted access to the network. The authentication process is managed by a central authentication server, which verifies the credentials provided by the client. This type of NAC solution provides granular control over network access and is commonly used in enterprise environments to provide secure access to corporate resources.

MAC filtering, on the other hand, is a simpler form of NAC that uses the Media Access Control (MAC) address of a device to control network access. A list of MAC addresses is maintained by the network administrator, and devices that are not on the list are blocked from accessing the network. While MAC filtering is easy to implement, it is not as secure as 802.1X, as MAC addresses can be easily spoofed, and it is also difficult to manage in large enterprise environments.

In summary, the key differences between 802.1X and MAC filtering are:

- 802.1X is an authentication protocol that uses EAP, while MAC filtering uses the MAC address of a device to control access.

- 802.1X provides granular control over network access, while MAC filtering provides a simple way to block unauthorized devices.

- 802.1X is more secure than MAC filtering, as MAC addresses can be easily spoofed.

- 802.1X is more difficult to manage in large enterprise environments than MAC filtering.

4.12   Can you explain the concept of DNSSEC, and why it is important for securing the DNS infrastructure?

The Domain Name System Security Extensions (DNSSEC) is a set of protocols that adds a layer of security to the Domain Name System (DNS) infrastructure. DNSSEC is designed to provide authentication and integrity for DNS data by using digital signatures and cryptographic key exchanges. DNSSEC enables clients to verify that the DNS responses they receive are authentic and have not been tampered with, thus preventing against DNS spoofing and other types of attacks on the DNS infrastructure.

DNSSEC works by adding digital signatures to each DNS record using public key cryptography. The digital signature is generated using the private key of the DNS zone, which is managed by the DNS administrator. The public key is then published in a DNS record called the DNSKEY record. DNS clients can obtain the DNSKEY record and use it to verify the signatures on the DNS records.

DNSSEC is important for securing the DNS infrastructure because the DNS is a critical component of the Internet's infrastructure, and it is often subject to attacks. DNS spoofing attacks are a common type of attack where an attacker tries to impersonate a legitimate DNS server by sending false DNS responses to clients. DNSSEC can prevent these types of attacks by providing clients with assurance that the DNS data they receive is authentic.

Another important aspect of DNSSEC is that it provides data integrity. Since each DNS record is signed using a digital signature, any modification to the record will invalidate the signature. Therefore, DNSSEC allows clients to detect any changes or modifications to DNS records that may indicate an attack.

In conclusion, DNSSEC is a crucial technology for securing the DNS infrastructure. It provides authentication, integrity, and confidentiality for DNS data, which is essential for reliable and secure operation of the Internet.

4.13 What is the purpose of Anycast, and how does it improve network performance and resilience?

Anycast is a networking technique where multiple devices or servers share the same IP address. When an anycast IP address is used, the data is routed to the nearest device or server based on the routing distance. The purpose of anycast is to improve network performance and resilience.

With anycast, the network can automatically redirect requests to the nearest device or server with the least number of hops, reducing latency and improving response time. For example, if a user sends a request to an anycast IP address for a website from New York, the router will route the request to the server nearest in New York. If the same request is sent from London, the router will route the request to the nearest server in London.

Anycast also improves network resilience by providing redundancy. If one device or server fails or goes offline, the anycast IP address can redirect the traffic to the next nearest device or server. This means that even if one device or server fails, the website or service will still be available to users. For example, a DNS server can use anycast addressing to ensure that its service is always available to users, even if one of its servers goes offline.

Another example of the use of anycast is in Content Delivery Networks (CDNs) where anycast IP addresses are commonly used to route users to the nearest data center. This reduces latency and improves service quality, resulting in faster page load times and a better user experience.

Overall, the purpose of anycast is to improve network performance and resilience by providing redundancy and directing traffic to the nearest device or server.

4.14   How does network automation and orchestration benefit network management and operations?

Network automation and orchestration are two key concepts that are transforming the way networks are managed and operated. Network automation involves using software tools and technologies to automate network configuration, provisioning, and management tasks, while network orchestration involves the coordination of different network components and services to deliver end-to-end network functions.

There are several benefits of network automation and orchestration for network management and operations, including:

1. Improved Efficiency: Automation and orchestration can help streamline network operations and reduce the response time for network requests, resulting in greater productivity and increased efficiency. By reducing manual intervention, the risk of human error also decreases, which in turn can help improve network reliability.

2. Increased Agility: Automation and orchestration help network administrators respond quickly to changes in the network environment. For example, automated provisioning can help deploy new network resources faster, while orchestration can help integrate new services and technologies seamlessly into existing network infrastructure.

3. Enhanced Visibility: Automation and orchestration tools provide real-time visibility into the network, enabling administrators to monitor network traffic, identify performance issues, and troubleshoot problems more quickly. This can help improve network uptime and reduce the time it takes to resolve network issues.

4. Simplified Management: Automation and orchestration can help simplify network management tasks by providing a single interface for administrators to manage the entire network. This can help reduce complexity and improve overall network performance.

Examples of automation and orchestration in action include:

1. A network operator can use automation tools such as Ansible or

Puppet to configure network switches and routers automatically. This can reduce the time and effort required to configure devices manually.

2. A network operator can use orchestration tools such as VMware NSX or OpenStack to provision network services automatically. This can help deploy new services more quickly and reduce the time it takes to modify existing services.

3. A network administrator can use automation tools to perform routine network maintenance tasks, such as software updates or backup and restore operations. This can help reduce downtime and improve network availability.

In conclusion, network automation and orchestration are key enablers for achieving a more efficient and agile network environment. By automating routine tasks and orchestrating network services, operators can simplify network management, improve network uptime, and deliver new services more quickly.

4.15 What is the role of Application Delivery Controllers (ADCs), and how do they help optimize application performance in a network?

Application Delivery Controllers (ADCs), also known as load balancers, are network devices that play a critical role in optimizing application performance for network users. ADCs are designed to act as intermediaries between servers and the client devices that are accessing the applications hosted on those servers. When a client device tries to access an application, the ADC intercepts the request, determines which server should respond, and forwards the request to that server. Once the server has processed the request, the ADC receives the response, inspects it, and delivers it back to the client device.

ADC devices help optimize application performance in several ways:

1. **Load balancing:** ADC devices use algorithms to distribute network traffic evenly across multiple servers, ensuring that no single

server becomes overwhelmed. By distributing network traffic in this way, ADC devices help to prevent server overloads that can lead to application slowdowns and downtime. Load balancing can be achieved at Layer 4 (Transport Layer) or Layer 7 (Application Layer) of the OSI model.

2. **Caching and Compression:** ADC devices can cache frequently accessed content and compress large files on the fly, reducing the amount of data that needs to be sent across the network. This results in faster application response times and improved user experience.

3. **SSL Offloading:** SSL (Secure Sockets Layer) encryption can be computationally expensive for servers. ADC devices can offload the SSL encryption process from servers, freeing up server resources and enabling them to process requests faster.

4. **Content Switching:** ADC devices can inspect network traffic to determine which content needs to be delivered to which client devices. This allows ADC devices to route specific types of traffic to specific servers, ensuring that each client receives the content or application that is best suited to its needs.

5. **Global Server Load Balancing (GSLB):** ADC devices with GSLB capabilities can distribute traffic across multiple geographically dispersed data centers. By keeping applications and content closer to users, this can provide faster response times and improved availability.

In conclusion, Application Delivery Controllers (ADCs) play a crucial role in optimizing application performance by distributing traffic, caching and compressing data, offloading SSL, content switching, and providing GSLB capabilities. By leveraging ADCs, organizations can improve application response times, enhance user experience, and reduce the risk of downtime.

4.16 Can you explain the difference between full mesh and partial mesh network architectures, and when you would use each?

In computer networking, mesh network architecture is a network topology where each node is connected to every other node. There are two types of mesh network architectures: full mesh and partial mesh.

In a full mesh network, every node is connected directly to every other node in the network. This type of network provides the highest level of redundancy and fault tolerance as data can be routed through multiple paths in case of a link failure. However, it requires more resources and is more expensive to implement due to the large number of connections required.

Partial mesh network, on the other hand, does not provide every node with a direct connection to every other node in the network. Instead, nodes are connected to only a subset of other nodes in the network. This type of network reduces the number of connections required, thus being more cost-effective than a full mesh network. However, it also reduces redundancy as some nodes may only have a single path to other parts of the network.

When considering the use of full mesh versus partial mesh network architectures, it is important to take into account the network's requirements, budget, and future scalability needs.

Full mesh networks are typically used in small-scale environments, such as computer clusters or data centers, where high availability and fault tolerance are paramount. For example, a small cluster of servers running critical applications may use a full mesh network topology to ensure that any server can communicate with any other server even if a link fails.

Partial mesh networks are more commonly used in larger networks, such as WANs or MANs, where the cost and complexity of implementing a full mesh network become prohibitive. For example, a large enterprise network may use a partial mesh architecture to connect different branches and data centers, with each branch only connected to a subset of other branches or data centers.

In conclusion, choosing the appropriate mesh network topology for a particular network depends on the network's size, requirement, and budget, as well as the level of fault tolerance, redundancy, and scalability required.

4.17 What are the key components and considerations for designing and implementing network security policies?

Designing and implementing network security policies is a critical process for any organization to protect its assets from various threats. A network security policy is a set of rules that govern access to network resources and communications. The following are the key components and considerations that organizations must consider when designing and implementing network security policies.

1. Risk Assessment The first step is to conduct a comprehensive risk assessment to identify the potential threats and vulnerabilities to the network. This helps to prioritize the security controls required to mitigate these risks.

2. Access Control Access control is a fundamental component of any network security policy. It ensures that only authorized users have access to sensitive resources. The policy should include guidelines for authentication, authorization, and accounting (AAA), such as the use of strong passwords, two-factor authentication, and user roles.

3. Encryption Encryption is crucial to safeguard data, especially when it is transmitted over an insecure network. Organizations must use secure protocols like SSL/TLS, and implement encryption for sensitive data such as passwords, credit card details, and other personal information.

4. Firewall Firewalls act as the first line of defense against external attacks. They monitor network traffic and filter out unauthorized access attempts. A well-designed network security policy should include guidelines for configuring firewall rules to protect against known and emerging threats.

5. Intrusion Detection and Prevention Intrusion detection and prevention systems (IDPS) are designed to detect and prevent attacks on the network. They monitor network traffic for suspicious activity and respond to potential threats in real-time. The policy should include guidelines for the deployment, management, and integration of IDPS with other security solutions.

6. Endpoint Security Endpoint security involves securing end-user devices such as desktops, laptops, and mobile devices. Organizations can implement security measures for endpoint security, such as antivirus, anti-malware, and host-based intrusion prevention systems (HIPS).

7. Security Incident Response The policy should also include a plan to respond to security incidents. Organizations should have clear procedures for reporting and responding to security incidents. They should have a dedicated incident response team and establish communication channels with external parties, such as law enforcement agencies, if necessary.

In conclusion, designing and implementing an effective network security policy involves a comprehensive approach that covers all the necessary security controls. Organizations must regularly review and update their security policies to adapt to evolving security threats, technologies, and best practices.

4.18 How do you troubleshoot network latency and packet loss issues effectively?

When troubleshooting network latency and packet loss issues, there are several steps that can be taken to identify the root cause of the problem and resolve it effectively.

1. Check for network congestion: If the network is experiencing con-

gestion, it can cause latency and packet loss. Use network monitoring tools to check for high bandwidth usage or network congestion. You can also use the 'ping' and 'traceroute' commands to check the path latency of packets.

2. Check for hardware issues: Faulty or outdated network hardware can cause network latency and packet loss. Check the physical devices such as routers, switches, and cables, to ensure they are functioning properly.

3. Check for software issues: Outdated or misconfigured software can also cause network latency and packet loss. Check the network configuration, such as MTU (maximum transmission unit), and ensure that they are configured properly.

4. Check for interference: Interference can also cause network latency and packet loss. Ensure that the network is not being interfered by other devices such as microwaves, cordless phones, or Bluetooth devices.

5. Use packet capture tools: Packet capture tools such as Wireshark can help identify packet loss and latency issues. Analyze the captured traffic to find errors and isolate the cause of the problem.

6. Check for network topology issues: Misconfigured network topology such as loops or incorrect spanning tree protocol configuration can cause network latency and packet loss. Ensure that the network topology is configured properly.

7. Check for security issues: Firewalls, antivirus software, or other security software can sometimes cause network latency and packet loss. Ensure that they are updated and correctly configured.

In summary, troubleshooting network latency and packet loss issues requires a systematic approach. By checking hardware and software, examining network topology, using packet capture and monitoring tools, and looking for interference or security issues, it is possible to isolate the root cause and resolve the issue effectively.

4.19 Can you explain the concept of network convergence, and why it is important for modern networking?

In computer networking, network convergence refers to the ability of various protocols, devices, and technologies to work together efficiently in order to deliver seamless and reliable network services. This means that data, voice, and video traffic can all be transmitted over the same network, and dynamically route traffic in the most efficient way possible.

Network convergence has become increasingly important in modern networking due to the growing number of devices and systems that are connected to the internet, as well as the rise of cloud-based services and applications. With so many different types of traffic traveling over the network, it is crucial for the network to be able to manage and prioritize the flow of data, optimizing performance and ensuring seamless connectivity.

One example of network convergence is the integration of voice and data networks in order to support Voice over Internet Protocol (VoIP) services. Traditionally, voice calls were transmitted over a separate network using specialized hardware and software. However, with the advent of VoIP, voice calls can now be transmitted over the same IP-based network as other types of data traffic. This convergence allows for more flexibility, cost savings, and ease of management.

Another example is the convergence between wired and wireless networks. In the past, wired and wireless networks were treated as separate infrastructures, with wired networks handling heavier traffic loads and wireless networks providing more mobility but with lower data rates. With the development of wireless technologies such as 5G, wireless networks are able to handle heavier loads and can now provide several gigabits per second of data rate. This convergence of wired and wireless networks allows for more dynamic and flexible network deployments, enabling better support for emerging applications that require low latency and high bandwidth.

Overall, network convergence is an essential concept in modern networking, allowing for efficient delivery of a wide variety of network services while improving performance, reliability, and management.

4.20   How does the concept of Intent-Based Networking (IBN) improve network management and operations?

Intent-Based Networking (IBN) is a revolutionary approach to network management and operations, which uses advanced automation and artificial intelligence (AI) technologies to manage and operate large, complex networks. In IBN, the network administrator specifies high-level business policies and objectives, and the network automatically translates those into specific configurations to optimize network performance, security, and compliance.

IBN improves network management and operations in several ways:

1. Automated network provisioning and configuration: IBN uses AI algorithms to automatically configure and provision network devices based on the administrator's intent. This reduces the amount of manual configuration needed, saving time and reducing errors.

2. Predictive network analytics: IBN continuously monitors network performance and behavior, analyzing data to identify potential issues before they become problems. This helps network administrators troubleshoot issues quickly and proactively plan for network scaling and growth.

3. Streamlined security management: IBN integrates security policies and protocols into the network, ensuring compliance with regulatory requirements and reducing the risk of breaches. It also uses machine learning algorithms to identify and respond to security threats in real-time, reducing the risk of data loss or damage.

4. Improved application performance: IBN optimizes network resources to ensure that critical applications receive the necessary bandwidth and prioritization. This reduces latency and improves application performance, enhancing the overall user experience.

For example, consider a healthcare organization that needs to secure patient data, while also ensuring fast and reliable network access for medical staff. With IBN, the administrator can specify a policy that says "secure patient data" and "provide fast network access for medical staff." The network would then automatically configure itself to meet these objectives, creating secure access controls and optimizing bandwidth allocation for staff applications.

Overall, IBN offers significant benefits for network management and operations, providing greater automation, intelligence, and agility to support evolving business needs.

Chapter 5

Expert

5.1 How do advanced routing techniques like policy-based routing and route redistribution work, and when should they be used?

Advanced routing techniques, such as policy-based routing (PBR) and route redistribution, are used to manipulate how network traffic is forwarded between different networks or subnets. They are commonly used in complex enterprise networks, where more granular control is required for traffic flow.

Policy-based Routing (PBR)

In traditional routing, traffic is forwarded based on the destination IP address, subnet mask, and a routing table lookup. However, with policy-based routing, traffic forwarding decisions are based on additional criteria, such as the source IP address, the protocol used, or the application-layer data. This allows for more granular control over which path traffic takes through the network.

PBR works by using a set of policies that define the conditions under which traffic is forwarded through a specific interface or next-hop router. These policies can be based on a range of attributes, such as source address, packet size, or application type. Once a policy is matched, PBR applies an alternative forwarding path, overriding the default routing table.

For example, a company may have multiple internet service providers (ISPs) with different bandwidths, latencies, and costs. PBR can be used to route traffic from specific subnets or applications through a particular ISP link based on policies such as cost, application type, or quality of service (QoS) requirements.

Route Redistribution

Route redistribution is another technique used to control traffic flow between different networks in a more granular way. It involves redistributing routes learned from one routing protocol into another. For example, a network may have routers running different routing protocols, such as OSPF and BGP. In such a scenario, route redistribution can be used to enable communication between networks running different protocols.

Route redistribution works by allowing one routing protocol to import network routes learned from another protocol. For example, the BGP protocol can be configured to import routes learned from OSPF, which can then be propagated throughout the BGP network. This enables more efficient use of network resources and allows for better traffic management.

For example, a company may have an e-commerce application running on a server connected to a LAN running OSPF, while their corporate website runs on a different server connected to a WAN running BGP. With route redistribution, the OSPF routes learned by the e-commerce application can be redistributed into BGP, allowing traffic to flow between the two networks.

When to Use Advanced Routing Techniques

Advanced routing techniques like PBR and route redistribution should be used in situations where more granular control over traffic flow is required. The decision to use these techniques depends on the complexity of the network, the requirements for traffic management, and the availability of resources.

For example, PBR can be used in networks where there are multiple WAN links and different QoS requirements for different applications. It can be used to ensure that specific applications are routed through the most appropriate link based on their QoS requirements.

Similarly, route redistribution can be used in networks where there are multiple routing protocols and the need to propagate routes between them. It can be used to ensure that routes learned from one protocol are available to other protocols, enabling more efficient use of network resources.

In summary, advanced routing techniques like PBR and route redistribution can provide more granular control over traffic flow in complex networks. They should be used when it is necessary to manage traffic based on specific criteria and when more efficient use of network resources is required.

5.2   Can you discuss the challenges of implementing and managing large-scale networks, and the solutions to overcome them?

Implementing and managing large-scale networks can pose numerous challenges. As the size and complexity of the network increases, so too do the difficulties that arise. Some of the main challenges are as follows:

1. Scalability: A large-scale network must be designed to accommodate growth in terms of number of users, devices and network traffic. This requires careful planning of network infrastructure, including switches and routers, to ensure that it can handle increasing demands. Additionally, network administrators must plan for scalability of network security measures, such as firewalls and intrusion detection systems.

Solution: A scalable network architecture that can adapt to changing needs is essential. Network administrators can use various technologies to address scalability issues including load balancing, clustering, virtualization, and cloud computing.

2. Security: As the size of the network increases, so too does the risk of security breaches. Large networks are more susceptible to cyber-attacks, and it becomes more challenging to ensure that all devices and users are properly secured. Maintaining data confidentiality, integrity, and availability is a significant challenge.

Solution: Implementing a comprehensive security strategy that encompasses all areas of the network is critical. This can include the use of firewalls, intrusion detection systems, encryption, access controls, and regular security audits.

3. Network Performance: In a large-scale network, network performance can be affected by factors such as network latency, bandwidth limitations, and packet loss. As the network grows in size, it becomes more challenging to maintain optimal network performance.

Solution: To maintain optimal network performance, administrators should implement network monitoring tools to measure network performance, identify bottlenecks, and proactively address issues. Additionally, using Quality of Service (QoS) mechanisms to prioritize different types of network traffic can help mitigate the impact of bandwidth limitations.

4. Network Management: As the size of the network grows, so too does the complexity of network management. Large-scale networks can be difficult to manage, particularly with regards to network configurations, device management, and network troubleshooting.

Solution: Network administrators can use network management tools to automate network configuration, device management and troubleshooting. Additionally, implementing network management policies and procedures can improve the efficiency of network management, such as documenting network configuration and change management processes.

In conclusion, implementing and managing large-scale networks can be a challenging task. However, by addressing the main challenges of scalability, security, network performance, and network management, network administrators can successfully manage large-scale networks with greater efficiency and effectiveness.

5.3 How do advanced network security technologies like micro-segmentation and zero-trust architecture work, and what are their benefits?

Advanced network security technologies like micro-segmentation and zero-trust architecture are rapidly gaining popularity due to the increased frequency and sophistication of cyber attacks. These technologies aim to enhance the security of networks by providing more granular control over access, reducing the attack surface, and improving visibility into network traffic.

Micro-segmentation is a technique used to divide a network into smaller segments, or subnets, to create multiple zones that can be isolated and secured independently. Each zone is protected by its own set of security controls, such as firewalls, intrusion detection systems, and access controls, which can be tailored to the specific needs of that zone. This approach minimizes the ability of attackers to move laterally within the network, as it requires them to compromise multiple security zones to gain access to sensitive assets.

For example, consider an e-commerce company that has several departments such as sales, marketing, and finance. Micro-segmentation can be used to create security zones for each department, where the security controls can be customized based on the specific needs of each department. In this way, even if one zone is compromised, the attackers would not be able to move laterally across other zones, protecting the sensitive information and assets of the entire organization.

Zero-trust architecture is a security model that assumes that all resources on a network are untrustworthy and must be verified before access is granted. This model requires that users and devices be authenticated and authorized before any network activity is allowed. In a zero-trust architecture, access to resources is tightly controlled and monitored, regardless of whether the resource is inside or outside the network perimeter.

For example, in a zero-trust architecture, a user who is trying to access a sensitive database would be required to go through multiple levels of authentication, such as multi-factor authentication, before they are granted access. This approach ensures that only authorized users are given access to sensitive resources, thereby reducing the likelihood of data breaches caused by unauthorized access.

The benefits of micro-segmentation and zero-trust architecture include enhanced security, reduced attack surface, increased visibility and auditability of network traffic, and the ability to deploy customized security controls to specific security zones. These technologies also facilitate compliance with regulatory requirements by providing granular control over access to sensitive data and assets.

In conclusion, micro-segmentation and zero-trust architecture are powerful security measures that can significantly enhance the security posture of an organization. By reducing the attack surface, providing more granular control over access, and improving visibility into network traffic, these technologies help organizations defend against increasingly complex cyber threats.

5.4   What are the key aspects to consider when planning and designing a network infrastructure for data centers and large enterprises?

When planning and designing a network infrastructure for data centers and large enterprises, there are several key aspects that should be considered to ensure the network can meet the organization's requirements, goals, and performance criteria:

1. Scalability - A network infrastructure should be scalable and able to handle future growth and expansion of the organization. This includes considering the number of users, devices, applications, and data that will be utilized.

2. Reliability - The network infrastructure should be highly reliable with minimal downtime or disruptions. This includes ensuring redundancy in critical components such as routers, switches, and servers.

3. Security - With increasing instances of cyber attacks and data

breaches, security should be a top priority in network infrastructure design. This includes implementing firewalls, intrusion detection systems, and secure access controls.

4. Performance - The network infrastructure should be designed to deliver high-performance and low-latency connectivity. This includes selecting the appropriate routing protocols, data transfer protocols, and network fabrics.

5. Virtualization - With the popularity of virtualization and cloud computing, the network infrastructure should be designed to accommodate virtual machine (VM) mobility and dynamic network provisioning.

6. Cost-effectiveness – While it is important to select high-quality networking equipment for reliability and performance, the infrastructure should be designed with cost-effectiveness in mind. This includes selecting equipment with an appropriate balance of price and performance.

7. Manageability - The network infrastructure should be easy to manage and monitor. This includes implementing network management systems and technologies to support automated monitoring and troubleshooting.

Overall, designing a network infrastructure for data centers and large enterprises requires careful consideration of several key aspects. Proper planning and design will allow organizations to achieve their business goals while ensuring reliability, scalability, performance, and security of their network.

5.5 Can you explain the challenges and solutions associated with network scalability, both horizontally and vertically?

Network scalability refers to the ability of a network to handle increasing amounts of data, users and devices in a flexible and efficient manner. This is important because as a business grows or as new technologies emerge, network demands increase, making it necessary to accommodate more data and users at a time.

There are two approaches to network scalability: horizontal scaling and vertical scaling.

Horizontal scaling involves adding more physical resources to a network, such as servers or switches, to increase its capacity. This approach is simple and cost-effective, but it has its limitations. For instance, adding more servers to a network may require additional IP addresses and result in issues with network congestion. Additionally, this approach does not always address all issues associated with scalability.

Vertical scaling, on the other hand, involves increasing the capacity of individual resources, such as servers or switches, to handle more data and users. This approach can be more expensive, but it also allows for more flexibility in addressing scalability issues and avoiding potential network congestion. However, vertical scaling has its own set of challenges, such as outgrowing the capacity of individual resources, leading to the need for frequent system upgrades.

Some challenges associated with network scalability include:

1. Limited bandwidth: Network bandwidth is crucial in determining the maximum amount of traffic a network can handle at a time. As more users and devices are added to a network, the available bandwidth may become limited, which can cause issues with network congestion and slow down data transfer rates.

2. Network complexity: As a network grows, it becomes more complex and harder to manage. Additional hardware and software can lead to more potential points of failure, making it more difficult to monitor and troubleshoot issues when they arise.

3. Security risks: As a network grows, so do the risks of security breaches. As more devices and users are added, there is greater potential for unauthorized access or data theft, which can lead to significant financial and reputational damage.

Some solutions to network scalability challenges include:

1. Implement load balancing techniques: Load balancing involves spreading network traffic across multiple resources to avoid network congestion and ensure that no single resource becomes overloaded. This technique can help avoid bottlenecks and keep the network running smoothly as it scales.

2. Implement network segmentation: Network segmentation involves dividing a network into smaller subnetworks or segments, each with its own security policies and access controls. This can help reduce the complexity of the network, limit the potential impact of security breaches and improve overall network performance.

3. Implement cloud-based solutions: Cloud-based solutions can help organizations quickly and easily scale their networks without the need for significant capital investments in hardware or infrastructure. These solutions often provide flexible, pay-as-you-go pricing models, making it easy to match network capacity to current demand.

In conclusion, network scalability is an essential aspect of any modern network infrastructure. Horizontal and vertical scaling offer different approaches to addressing scalability issues, and implementing load balancing techniques, network segmentation, and cloud-based solutions can help organizations overcome the challenges associated with scalability.

5.6 How does Software-Defined Networking (SDN) impact network management, and what are its potential advantages and drawbacks?

Software-Defined Networking (SDN) is a paradigm shift in network architecture that decouples the control plane and data plane in network devices, centralizing network management and improving network programmability. In traditional networking, network devices integrate the control plane and data plane, which means that they have to perform both packet forwarding and control functions. On the other hand, SDN separates the control plane from the data plane, allowing network administrators to manage network devices from a centralized controller, while the switching and forwarding functions are left to the data plane.

The impact of SDN on network management is profound. Instead of configuring network devices individually, network administrators can define network policies centrally from a single point of management through an SDN controller. This approach greatly simplifies network management, reduces configuration errors, and enhances network operations capabilities. For instance, when a network administrator needs to update routing policies, Quality of Service (QoS) protocols, or firewall rules, they don't have to manually configure individual network devices, but can apply the policies across the network using the SDN controller. Moreover, since network function virtualization is the underpinning concept of SDN, network administrators can deploy new network functions and services using software-defined network functions.

The advantages of SDN include:

1. Greater network flexibility - With software-defined networks, the network administrator can dynamically adjust the network configuration to accommodate changes in traffic or services.

2. Improved network security - SDN makes network security features such as firewalls and intrusion detection systems more robust by facilitating centralized policy management and enforcement of access control rules.

3. Faster network provisioning - SDN accelerates the deployment of network services and reduces time to market by abstracting complex network protocols and configurations from the deployment process.

Despite its advantages, there are a few potential drawbacks of SDN, which include:

1. The need for more advanced skills - SDN requires network administrators to master new skills such as programming and software development. This can pose challenges, especially for organizations with traditional network architectures that lack software engineering capabilities.

2. Increased reliance on the SDN controller - SDN relies heavily on the SDN controller, which can become a single point of failure. Therefore,

organizations must ensure that the controller is always available and secure.

3. Security vulnerabilities - Since SDN relies heavily on software, it may increase the risk of security vulnerabilities. Organizations must take appropriate steps to secure their SDN controllers and networks by updating their software regularly, implementing authentication and encryption mechanisms, and using intrusion detection systems.

In conclusion, SDN has revolutionized the way networks are managed, allowing for added flexibility, scalability, and security. However, it also presents its own set of potential drawbacks and can require additional skills from network administrators transitioning from traditional network architecture to SDN.

5.7 Can you discuss the role of network analytics and telemetry in network performance monitoring and optimization?

Network analytics and telemetry are critical tools in network performance monitoring and optimization, providing insights into network behaviors and trends that can help network administrators identify and troubleshoot issues more quickly and effectively.

Network analytics involves the use of data gathering, analysis, and visualization tools to gain insights into network performance and behavior. It enables network administrators to collect metrics such as packet loss, latency, jitter, bandwidth utilization, and other key performance indicators (KPIs) across the network, and then analyze this data to identify trends, patterns, and anomalies that can affect network performance.

Telemetry, on the other hand, involves the real-time monitoring and reporting of network data, providing network administrators with immediate visibility into network conditions and issues as they happen. Through the use of telemetry systems, network administrators can capture and analyze real-time data on network traffic, device status, and other critical network parameters.

Together, network analytics and telemetry provide a powerful set of tools for network performance monitoring and optimization. By capturing and analyzing a wide range of network data, these tools enable network administrators to gain deeper insights into network performance, troubleshoot issues more quickly, and optimize network performance to meet the needs of the organization.

For example, network analytics and telemetry can help network administrators identify issues such as congestion, packet loss, and latency spikes that can degrade network performance. By analyzing data on network traffic flows and device status, administrators can pinpoint the source of these issues and take corrective action to mitigate their impact.

Similarly, network analytics and telemetry can help administrators optimize network performance by identifying areas where bandwidth utilization is high or QoS policies are not being properly applied. By analyzing this data, administrators can adjust network configurations to ensure that traffic is prioritized appropriately and bandwidth is allocated efficiently.

Overall, network analytics and telemetry are critical tools in network performance monitoring and optimization, providing network administrators with the data and insights they need to optimize network performance and ensure that the network can meet the needs of the organization.

5.8   What is the importance of network resilience and disaster recovery planning, and how can it be achieved effectively?

Network resilience and disaster recovery planning are crucial aspects of computer networking as they help organizations to respond effectively to disruptive events such as natural disasters, cyber-attacks, and network failures. Network resilience is the ability of a network to withstand and recover from unexpected disruptions, without significant impact on network performance, while disaster recovery is the process of restoring network resources after a disruption has occurred.

The importance of network resilience and disaster recovery planning cannot be overstated. Without proper planning, an organization's network can be vulnerable to unpredictable events that can lead to significant financial losses, damage to reputation, and potential security breaches. Additionally, several legal and regulatory requirements, such as the General Data Protection Regulation (GDPR), require organizations to have disaster recovery plans in place to ensure the protection of sensitive data.

To achieve effective network resilience and disaster recovery planning, several key considerations should be taken into account, including:

1. Risk assessment: Conducting a detailed analysis of the risks that may affect the network, and prioritizing them based on their potential impact and likelihood of occurrence. The risk assessment should consider both internal and external threats to the network.

2. Network design: Developing a network design that incorporates redundancy, backup systems, and failover mechanisms to reduce the impact of disruptions on network operations. This includes using technologies such as load balancers, backup servers, and cloud-based services to provide backup and recovery capabilities.

3. Disaster recovery plan: Developing a comprehensive disaster recovery plan that outlines the steps to be taken during and after a disruption to restore the network to its normal state. The plan should define roles and responsibilities, identify critical resources, and prioritize recovery activities.

4. Testing: Regular testing of the disaster recovery plan to ensure that it is effective and up-to-date. Testing should include simulations of various disaster scenarios, and identifying any gaps or weaknesses that need to be addressed.

5. Training: Providing regular training to network administrators, IT staff, and employees on disaster recovery procedures, and ensuring that they are familiar with the processes and tools required to respond to disruptions.

In conclusion, network resilience and disaster recovery planning are critical aspects of computer networking, and should be given serious consideration by all organizations. Implementing effective network resilience and disaster recovery measures can help to mitigate the impact of disruptions, ensure the continuity of network operations, and safeguard sensitive data.

5.9 How do emerging networking technologies like 5G, IoT, and edge computing impact network design and management?

Emerging networking technologies, such as 5G, IoT, and edge computing, are significantly changing network design and management. These technologies are driven by the increasing demand for reliable and high-speed connectivity, optimization of resource utilization, and real-time decision-making. Let's discuss the impact of each technology on network design and management.

5G:

5G technology introduces new network topologies, such as network slicing, which allows the creation of multiple virtual networks on a common physical infrastructure. To facilitate the deployment of 5G networks, network design and management must adapt to support the higher bandwidth, lower latency, and massive number of devices. With 5G, network operators must deploy small cells with high-frequency antennas closer to the end-users to ensure seamless connectivity. This requires new designs to support these small cells' deployment and management. Additionally, 5G introduces massive Machine-Type Communications (mMTC) from connected devices, such as autonomous cars, smart cities, and Industry 4.0 applications. This introduces new challenges of managing the resources for these services while keeping the network stable.

IoT:

IoT devices introduce new requirements for network design and management. IoT devices demand low-power connectivity, security, and scalability to support millions of connected devices. Network design and management need to allow for easy integration of IoT devices while ensuring a secure environment. The network must be capable of processing vast amounts of data generated by IoT devices and support real-time decision-making. The rise in IoT devices also calls for the deployment of edge computing technologies to reduce latency and improve reaction times.

Edge computing:

Edge computing is an emerging technology designed to bring processing capabilities and data storage closer to the end-users to provide faster and more efficient responses. This requires a new network design that distributes resources between the central cloud and the edge of the network. Edge computing can help reduce network latency and decrease the amount of traffic sent over the network, thus improving the overall network performance. The management of edge computing resources depends on the computational tasks and determining where to process them - edge, cloud or device.

In conclusion, emerging networking technologies such as 5G, IoT, and edge computing provide significant benefits to network design and management. These technologies present new challenges in terms of deployment and management, but they also provide opportunities to enhance the network's performance, scalability, and reliability. As always, expert knowledge is required to ensure smooth integration of these technologies into the network infrastructure.

5.10 What are the key challenges in implementing and managing multi-cloud and hybrid cloud network environments?

Multi-cloud and hybrid cloud networks are becoming increasingly popular due to the flexibility, scalability, and cost savings they offer. However, implementing and managing such environments present several challenges that need to be addressed for the successful deployment and operation of a multi-cloud or hybrid cloud solution.

1. Network Complexity: One of the biggest challenges in managing multi-cloud and hybrid cloud networks is the increased complexity of the network. In a hybrid cloud environment, multiple cloud providers and on-premises infrastructure are interconnected through a network, creating a complex mesh of connections that must be managed. Multi-cloud networks face a similar challenge, with multiple cloud providers connected through a network that must be secured and managed.

2. Network Security: Multi-cloud and hybrid cloud networks pose significant security challenges due to their distributed nature. Each cloud provider has its own set of security controls, which need to be coordinated and configured to ensure that the overall network is secure. Moreover, data must be secured during transmission between the different cloud providers and on-premises infrastructure. This requires careful planning and implementation of security policies, access controls, and encryption mechanisms.

3. Network Visibility and Control: When a network spans multiple clouds and on-premises environments, it becomes difficult to maintain visibility and control over the entire network. Network administrators need to have visibility into the performance, health, and security of the entire network to ensure that it is operating at peak efficiency. This requires a comprehensive monitoring and management solution that can provide end-to-end visibility across the entire network.

4. Application Performance: Multi-cloud and hybrid cloud environments can impact application performance due to network latency, bandwidth limitations, and other factors. Applications must be optimized for the distributed nature of the network, ensuring that they are designed to operate efficiently across multiple clouds and on-premises infrastructure. This requires careful planning and optimization of application architecture, network topology, and performance tuning.

5. Interoperability: Different cloud providers may have different APIs, standards, and protocols, making it difficult to ensure interoperability between different cloud providers and on-premises infrastructure. This requires careful evaluation and selection of cloud providers, as well as careful planning and implementation of integration mechanisms that can ensure that applications and data can be seamlessly migrated between different cloud providers.

In summary, implementing and managing multi-cloud and hybrid cloud network environments require a comprehensive approach that takes into consideration several factors, including network complexity, security, visibility and control, application performance, and interoperability. Careful planning and implementation of solutions to address these challenges are essential for the successful deployment and operation of a multi-cloud or hybrid cloud solution.

5.11   Can you discuss the role of network programmability, APIs, and network function virtualization (NFV) in modern networking?

In modern networking, network programmability, APIs, and network function virtualization (NFV) all play critical roles in shaping the way networks function to meet the ever-increasing bandwidth and latency demands of contemporary applications.

Network Programmability refers to the ability of network devices to be remotely managed and configured using software programming interfaces (APIs) that lessen the burden on manual configuration. With programmable networks, areas of a network can be automatically configured and self-tuned for the best performance possible. The key advantage of a software-built network is that it permits reuse and abstracts the implementation details of network devices, which means that network administrators can focus on the business needs of an organization instead of the underlying hardware configuration.

Automation and orchestration of system resources enable IT teams to increase efficiency, reduce costs, save time and minimize human error. By integrating APIs into network topology, automated network programmability eliminates the need for manual modifications and configurations, which can be time-consuming and prone to errors.

APIs are the language that enables network programmability. They empower automation tools and network management systems to interconnect and communicate with various data centres and applications, enabling a network to function efficiently without manual intervention. An API is an interface used to build applications that integrate with other applications (or web services). It is software-to-software interaction, not user-to-software interaction because users are only theoretically using the front-end of the app rather than interacting with the back-end database directly.

NFV is a network architecture that replaces dedicated hardware with virtual instances of network functions using software infrastructure designed on standard servers, switches, and storage environments. Network functions can be virtualized through software, which enables network administrators to run them on common server hardware. With NFV, several network functions can be stacked together and deployed in software, running on the same server hardware, rather than as separate hardware appliances with dedicated functionality.

A significant advantage of network virtualization is that it allows hardware resources to be shared, providing more versatility and flexibility for an organization's network configuration. Virtualization enables self-provisioning, which means that as soon as a new server is needed, it can automatically be provisioned to handle processes as the company scales by deploying the needed software on the infrastructure.

In conclusion, network programmability enables the configuration of the network, while APIs facilitate the integration between applications and other tools, and NFV virtualizes the hardware that powers the network. The combination of these technologies permits unparalleled efficiency in the development and management of modern networks, enabling IT teams to increase agility while reducing costs and minimizing human errors.

5.12   What are the key considerations when planning and implementing Quality of Service (QoS) policies in a network with diverse traffic requirements?

Quality of Service (QoS) is an important aspect of network design and implementation, especially in networks with diverse traffic requirements. Here are the key considerations when planning and implementing QoS policies in such networks:

1. Traffic Analysis: It is critical to analyze the traffic in the network to determine the type of traffic flows and their respective requirements. Traffic analysis helps to identify the various traffic types, such as real-time traffic (e.g., voice and video), interactive traffic (e.g., web browsing and instant messaging), and bulk data traffic (e.g., file transfers and backups). Each traffic type has different QoS requirements, and the QoS policies must be designed to accommodate these differences.

2. Priority and Classification: Once the traffic types in the network have been identified, the next step is to assign them priority levels and classify them based on their QoS requirements. Traffic classification is important because it enables the network devices to differentiate between different types of traffic and apply the appropriate QoS policies. Prioritization is typically done using a set of predefined levels, such as high, medium, and low, and policies are defined accordingly.

3. Bandwidth Allocation: Bandwidth allocation is a crucial aspect of QoS implementation, especially in networks with diverse traffic requirements. It involves assigning a specific amount of bandwidth to each traffic type or priority level based on its requirements. For instance, real-time traffic such as voice and video requires a low-latency, high-bandwidth connection, so they will be allocated a higher percentage of the network bandwidth.

4. Queuing and Scheduling: Queuing and scheduling mechanisms ensure that packets are processed in a timely and efficient manner, and this is critical for ensuring good QoS in networks with diverse traffic requirements. Different queuing and scheduling algorithms can be used for different traffic types or priority levels. For example, strict priority queuing can be used for real-time traffic, while weighted fair queuing can be used for bulk data traffic.

5. Network Monitoring: Network monitoring is important for ensuring that the QoS policies are functioning as intended. It involves tracking the performance of the network devices, measuring the traffic flows, and analyzing the effectiveness of the QoS policies in meeting the traffic requirements. Network monitoring tools such as SNMP (Simple Network Management Protocol) can be used to provide real-time visibility into the network performance and help troubleshoot

any issues.

In summary, successful implementation of QoS policies in networks with diverse traffic requirements requires a comprehensive understanding of the traffic types, their QoS requirements, and the network infrastructure. Prioritization, classification, bandwidth allocation, queuing, scheduling, and network monitoring are all critical components of a well-designed QoS policy.

5.13 How do advanced traffic engineering techniques like Resource Reservation Protocol (RSVP) and Constraint-Based Routing work?

Resource Reservation Protocol (RSVP) and Constraint-Based Routing (CBR) are advanced traffic engineering techniques used in computer networking to control network traffic flows and provide Quality of Service (QoS) guarantees for network applications.

RSVP is a signaling protocol that is used by network devices to request and reserve the necessary network resources to support a specific traffic flow. RSVP works by sending messages known as RSVP PATH and RSVP RESV messages to the devices along the path of a traffic flow. The RSVP PATH message is used to request the necessary network resources, while the RSVP RESV message is used to reserve the resources requested by the PATH message. These messages propagate through the network to all devices that are along the path of the traffic flow. The devices that receive the RSVP PATH message reserve the necessary network resources and respond with a RSVP RESV message indicating that the resources have been successfully reserved.

CBR is a routing technique that ensures that the traffic flows along a particular path of the network that meets certain constraints or requirements. CBR works by using a path computation algorithm that computes a path for each traffic flow that satisfies the constraints specified by the QoS requirements of the application. These constraints can include things like bandwidth requirements, delay requirements, or jitter requirements. Once the path computation algorithm has computed the path for the traffic flow, the network devices use the RSVP protocol to reserve the necessary resources for that path.

Here's an example of how RSVP and CBR could be used together to provide QoS guarantees for a video streaming application. Let's say that a user is streaming a high-definition video on their computer. The video stream requires a minimum bandwidth of 10 Mbps and must be delivered with less than 100 ms of delay. The network administrator has configured the network to use CBR to calculate the optimal path for the video stream based on the QoS requirements. The CBR algorithm calculates a path that satisfies the requirements, and the network devices use the RSVP protocol to reserve the necessary resources to support the video stream. As a result, the video stream is delivered to the user with the required bandwidth and delay guarantees, providing a high-quality viewing experience. If the network resources become congested, the RSVP protocol can dynamically adjust the resource reservation to ensure that the QoS requirements for the video stream are still satisfied.

5.14   Can you explain the concept of SD-WAN, and how it is used to optimize wide area network performance and management?

SD-WAN (Software-Defined Wide Area Network) is a technology that is transforming the world of WANs by improving network performance and management. It is essentially an intelligent and application-aware overlay on a WAN that can enable multiple transport technologies, such as broadband internet, LTE, and MPLS, to work together seamlessly.

The main purpose of SD-WAN is to improve network performance by providing more flexible and intelligent path selection, reducing network congestion and packet loss, and ensuring reliable and secure transmission of data across the WAN. With SD-WAN, IT administrators can easily manage and prioritize network traffic based on their criticality and bandwidth requirements, providing a better user experience and optimal utilization of network resources.

SD-WAN uses centralized policy-based management along with intelligent and predictive analytics to simplify network configuration and monitoring, making it easier to deploy, manage, and troubleshoot network issues. SD-WAN appliances spread throughout the network continuously collect performance data and report any anomalies, which the IT team can review and address proactively to minimize the risk of downtime or degraded service levels.

SD-WAN can also provide a much-needed boost to security by implementing end-to-end encryption, advanced threat prevention, and compliance with regulatory requirements. It can enable secure and direct access to cloud applications, eliminating the backhaul traffic that passes through the data center.

One of the biggest advantages of SD-WAN is that it can reduce WAN costs significantly. By leveraging broadband and other cost-effective internet links, SD-WAN allows organizations to augment their expensive MPLS circuits and reduce their dependence on them. This results in reduced WAN costs and faster ROI.

In summary, SD-WAN is a transformative technology that is changing the face of wide area networking by improving performance, simplifying management, ensuring security, and reducing costs. It is a smart investment for organizations looking to optimize their WANs and deliver a better user experience.

5.15   What is the role of network forensics and threat hunting in maintaining network security and incident response?

Network forensics and threat hunting are two essential components of network security and incident response. Network forensics involves collecting and analyzing network traffic data to investigate security incidents, while threat hunting involves proactively searching for and identifying potential security threats.

The role of network forensics in maintaining network security is twofold. First, network forensics can be used to investigate security incidents and determine the root cause of the incident. This involves collecting and analyzing network traffic data to identify the source of the attack, the attack vector, and the extent of the damage caused by the attack. Network forensics can also be used to collect evidence that can be presented in court if legal action is taken.

Secondly, network forensics can be used to enhance network security by identifying potential vulnerabilities and weaknesses in the network. By analyzing network traffic data, network forensics experts can identify patterns of behavior that may indicate an attack is imminent, or identify vulnerabilities that can be exploited by attackers. This allows network administrators to take proactive steps to mitigate these risks before they are exploited.

Threat hunting, on the other hand, involves proactively searching for and identifying potential security threats. This involves collecting and analyzing vast amounts of data from various sources, including network traffic data, security logs, and threat intelligence feeds. By using advanced analytical tools and techniques, threat hunters can identify suspicious behavior within the network, such as unusual traffic patterns, unauthorized access attempts, or anomalies in system logs.

The role of threat hunting in maintaining network security lies in its ability to detect and mitigate threats before they cause significant damage. By identifying and responding to potential threats in real-time, threat hunting can help prevent data breaches, network downtime, and financial losses. Threat hunting can also be used to identify areas where network security can be improved, such as by implementing new security protocols or updating existing defenses.

In conclusion, network forensics and threat hunting are critical components of network security and incident response. By using advanced analytical techniques and tools, and by collecting and analyzing vast amounts of data, network forensics experts and threat hunters can identify potential security threats, investigate security incidents, and prevent future attacks.

5.16   How do advanced DNS features like DNS Load Balancing and DNS-based DDoS mitigation work, and when should they be used?

Advanced DNS features, such as DNS Load Balancing and DNS-based DDoS mitigation, are used to improve the performance and security of websites and applications. In this answer, we will discuss each of these features and how they work.

DNS Load Balancing

DNS Load Balancing is a technique used to distribute traffic across multiple servers, also known as a server farm or a server pool. This distribution helps to improve the availability, scalability, and performance of web applications.

When using DNS Load Balancing, a DNS server will return multiple IP addresses for a single hostname. Each IP address corresponds to a different server in the server farm, and incoming requests are distributed across these servers. This distribution ensures that no single server is overwhelmed with traffic, leading to faster response times and higher availability.

DNS Load Balancing can be implemented with various load balancing algorithms, such as round-robin, least-connections, and IP-hash. Round-robin distributes traffic evenly across servers, while least-connections directs traffic to the server with the fewest active connections. IP-hash uses a hashing algorithm based on the client's IP address to determine which server to direct traffic to.

DNS load balancing is commonly used in high-traffic websites and applications to distribute incoming traffic across multiple servers, thereby improving the website or application's performance and reducing downtime.

DNS-based DDoS Mitigation

DNS-based DDoS mitigation is a technique used to protect networks and applications from Distributed Denial of Service (DDoS) attacks.

DDoS attacks attempt to overwhelm a network or server with traffic from multiple sources, rendering it unavailable to legitimate users.

DNS-based DDoS mitigation works by redirecting traffic to a cloud-based DNS infrastructure that can filter out malicious traffic before it reaches the targeted server or network. The cloud-based infrastructure can automatically detect and remove traffic from known sources of malicious traffic, such as botnets, while still allowing legitimate traffic to pass through.

To use DNS-based DDoS mitigation, a DNS server can be configured to redirect all traffic to a cloud-based DNS infrastructure during an attack. This redirection allows the cloud-based infrastructure to monitor and filter the traffic, while still providing the IP address of the targeted server or network to legitimate users. Once the attack is over, traffic can be directed back to the targeted server or network.

DNS-based DDoS mitigation is commonly used in organizations that are at a high risk of DDoS attacks, such as financial institutions, government agencies, and large e-commerce websites.

In summary, DNS Load Balancing and DNS-based DDoS mitigation are advanced DNS features used to improve website performance and security. DNS Load Balancing distributes traffic across multiple servers to improve availability and scalability, while DNS-based DDoS mitigation protects networks and applications from DDoS attacks. These features should be used in organizations that require high levels of website performance and security, such as e-commerce websites, financial institutions, and government agencies.

5.17   Can you discuss the importance of network compliance and regulatory requirements in network design and management?

Network compliance and regulatory requirements are critical factors in the design and management of any computer network. Compliance and regulatory requirements refer to the legal and industry standards that govern the use and management of information systems, including data privacy, security, and confidentiality. Failure to comply with these requirements can have severe legal, financial, and reputational consequences for an organization. Therefore, network designers and managers must take extra care to ensure that their networks meet these compliance and regulatory requirements.

There are several reasons why network compliance and regulatory requirements are so important:

1. Compliance with legal requirements: Various laws govern how data is collected, used, and stored by organizations. For example, in the United States, the Gramm-Leach-Bliley Act (GLBA) and the Health Insurance Portability and Accountability Act (HIPAA) regulate how financial institutions and healthcare organizations manage customer data. Failure to comply with these laws can result in heavy fines and legal action against the organization.

2. Protection of sensitive data: Compliance and regulatory requirements often exist to protect sensitive data such as personal and financial information. Designing and managing networks that comply with these requirements ensures that sensitive data remains protected and cannot be accessed or stolen by unauthorized parties.

3. Maintain customer trust: Compliance with regulatory requirements can help an organization maintain its customers' trust. By demonstrating that it takes data privacy and security seriously, an organization can build a reputation for being reliable, trustworthy, and responsible.

4. Avoid reputational damage: Non-compliance with regulatory requirements can lead to significant reputational damage for an organization. In today's interconnected world, news of a data breach can spread rapidly and damage an organization's reputation in the eyes of its customers, partners, and the general public.

To ensure compliance and regulatory requirements are met, network designers and managers must keep up with the latest legal and industry standards. They must design their networks to meet these requirements, implement appropriate security measures, and monitor their systems for any potential vulnerabilities that may arise. They must also train their staff to be aware of the importance of compliance and regulatory requirements and to ensure that any changes to the regulations are quickly taken into account.

Overall, compliance and regulatory requirements play a critical role in the design and management of networks, and failure to comply can have severe legal, financial, and reputational consequences. By ensuring that networks comply with these requirements, organizations can protect sensitive data, maintain customer trust, and avoid reputational damage.

5.18 What are the challenges of managing and securing wireless networks, particularly in large-scale and high-density environments?

Wireless networks have become prevalent in many environments due to their flexibility and convenience. However, managing and securing such networks can be a complex task, especially in large-scale and high-density environments. Here are some of the key challenges that network administrators face in managing and securing wireless networks:

1. Interference: Wireless networks operate on unlicensed radio frequencies, which are subject to interference from other wireless devices and environmental factors. In high-density environments, such as airports, stadiums, or office buildings, multiple wireless access points (APs) can cause interference, resulting in signal degradation and slow network performance.

2. Bandwidth constraints: Wireless networks have limited bandwidth compared to wired networks. In high-density environments, where many users are trying to access the network at the same time, bandwidth constraints can lead to slow connections and network congestion.

3. Security threats: Wireless networks are vulnerable to a variety of security threats, including unauthorized access, eavesdropping, and denial-of-service (DoS) attacks. In high-density environments, the

risk of these threats is amplified due to the increased number of devices and users on the network.

4. Device diversity: In a large-scale wireless network, there may be a wide range of devices with different operating systems, security profiles, and connectivity requirements. Managing compatibility and ensuring security for all devices can be a significant challenge.

5. Scalability: As the number of users and devices on a wireless network increases, managing and maintaining the network becomes more complex. Administrators must ensure that the network infrastructure can handle the increased load and is scalable to accommodate future growth.

To address these challenges, network administrators can implement several best practices for managing and securing wireless networks in high-density environments. These include:

1. Implementing a centralized network management system that can monitor and manage multiple APs from a single location.

2. Conducting periodic site surveys to identify sources of interference and optimize AP placement for maximum coverage and performance.

3. Implementing strong authentication and encryption protocols to prevent unauthorized access and protect data in transit.

4. Implementing bandwidth management techniques such as Quality of Service (QoS) policies to ensure that critical applications receive priority over less important ones.

5. Regularly auditing the network infrastructure and devices to identify and remediate security vulnerabilities.

By following these best practices, network administrators can help ensure the performance, security, and scalability of wireless networks in large-scale and high-density environments.

5.19 How do advanced network management tools like AI and machine learning help in optimizing network performance and security?

Advanced network management tools such as AI and machine learning have revolutionized how we manage and optimize network performance and security.

In terms of network performance, AI and machine learning can be used to analyze vast amounts of network data and provide intelligent insights that help identify and address network bottlenecks, compatibility issues, and performance degradation. For example, AI algorithms can analyze network traffic patterns and identify the root causes of network issues, such as latency or packet loss.

One of the benefits of using AI and machine learning for network performance optimization is that it enables networks to be optimized proactively, rather than reactively. AI and machine learning algorithms can be trained to recognize patterns and anticipate potential network issues before they become serious problems. By identifying potential issues and providing early warning signs, network administrators can proactively take steps to optimize network performance and avoid downtime.

Another area where AI and machine learning are being used to optimize network performance is in the field of network automation. Network automation tools leverage AI and machine learning algorithms to automate network configuration, management, and security tasks. This helps to save time and resources for network administrators, who can focus on more strategic tasks such as planning and troubleshooting.

When it comes to network security, AI and machine learning are becoming increasingly important as threats become more sophisticated and complex. By using machine learning to analyze network traffic patterns, AI algorithms can identify and block threats in real-time, reducing the risk of cyber attacks or data breaches. For example, AI and machine learning algorithms can be used to identify anomalous network traffic patterns and take corrective action in real-time, preventing potential security breaches.

In addition to threat detection and prevention, AI and machine learning algorithms can also be used for security monitoring and compliance reporting. By analyzing network data in real-time, AI and machine learning can help identify potential security vulnerabilities and provide alerts to network administrators. Additionally, AI and machine learning algorithms can be used to generate detailed security reports and compliance data, which helps organizations stay compliant with industry regulations and standards.

In conclusion, AI and machine learning are powerful tools that can greatly enhance network performance and security. By using advanced algorithms to analyze network data, these tools can help network administrators identify and address performance issues proactively and mitigate security threats in real-time. By leveraging the power of AI and machine learning, organizations can optimize their network infrastructure and ensure that their network is secure and compliant with industry regulations and standards.

5.20   Can you explain the concept of network slicing in 5G, and how it can be used to create tailored network experiences for different use cases?

Network slicing is a concept in 5G that allows the creation of virtual, customized networks on top of a common physical infrastructure. It enables the partitioning of the network into independent "slices" with unique size, configuration, and functionality.

Each slice is configured with specific network characteristics such as latency, data rate, capacity, security, and reliability, based on the specific requirements of the use case. By creating a dedicated slice for a particular use case, network operators can ensure that the network is optimized for that particular use case, providing tailored network experiences for the users.

For example, a network slice can be created for a self-driving car.

This slice can be configured to provide low latency and ultra-reliable connectivity to ensure that the car can make quick and accurate decisions based on the data it receives from the network. Additionally, the slice can be designed to provide high bandwidth and low packet loss to support the large amounts of data generated by the car's sensors.

Another example is a network slice for virtual reality (VR) applications. This slice can be optimized for high throughput and low latency to ensure smooth and responsive VR experiences without any lag or buffering. Additionally, the slice can be designed to ensure high data rates to support the large amounts of data required for VR applications.

In summary, network slicing is a powerful concept that enables the creation of customized networks that are optimized for specific use cases. By leveraging network slicing in 5G, network operators can provide tailored network experiences to their users, enabling new and innovative applications that were not possible in previous generations of cellular networks.

Chapter 6

Guru

6.1 Can you discuss the challenges and solutions associated with network protocol and infrastructure evolution, such as the transition from IPv4 to IPv6?

With the increasing demands for real-time multimedia applications and exponential growth in the number of devices being connected to the Internet, it has become necessary to make several improvements to the existing network infrastructure and protocols to support such demands. This evolution of network infrastructure and protocols comes with a set of challenges that need to be addressed. One such significant challenge is the transition from IPv4 to IPv6.

IPv4 is the current version of the Internet Protocol in use, and it has been utilized for a long period. However, the number of devices connected to the Internet has significantly increased over the years, and IPv4 was not designed to handle these numbers. IPv4 has a limited address space of only 32 bits, which translates to approximately 4.3 billion possible unique addresses. Given the current rate of adoption, the exhaustion of IPv4 addresses was inevitable. As a solution, the IPv6 protocol was introduced in 1998, which uses 128-bit addresses, which provides a virtually unlimited address space.

One of the major challenges associated with the transition from IPv4 to IPv6 is the incompatibility between the two protocols. IPv4 and IPv6 packets are not mutually understood, and a device that only supports one of the protocols would not understand a packet sent in the other protocol. Therefore, it is necessary to build a bridge between the two protocols to enable communication between devices that use different protocols.

One solution to this challenge is the use of dual-stack architecture, which involves maintaining both IPv4 and IPv6 protocol stacks on networking hardware such as switches, routers, and end-systems, to enable communication between different devices. This approach can also be extended to network applications, where applications can support both IPv4 and IPv6 protocols.

Another solution is the use of tunneling, a technique that encapsulates the IPv6 packets inside IPv4 packets and vice versa, thereby enabling older devices that support only IPv4 to communicate with devices that use IPv6. However, tunneling adds overhead, which leads to reduced performance in the network.

Another challenge associated with the transition from IPv4 to IPv6 is the limited support for IPv6 in older networking equipment, such as switches and routers. To address this, networking vendors need to update their devices to support IPv6 fully or create new devices that support both protocols.

To conclude, the transition from IPv4 to IPv6 presents significant challenges, including protocol incompatibility, support for older network devices, and the potential reduction of network performance, among others. However, there are solutions such as dual-stack architecture, tunneling, and updating networking equipment to support IPv6, which can mitigate these challenges.

6.2 How do advanced network architecture concepts like Segment Routing and Information-Centric Networking (ICN) impact network design and performance?

Segment Routing and Information-Centric Networking (ICN) are two advanced networking concepts that have the potential to significantly impact network design and performance.

Segment Routing is a network architecture that simplifies the creation of paths through the network by allowing packets to be forwarded along pre-defined paths, or segments, rather than relying on complex routing protocols. This approach offers a number of benefits, including improved network scalability, reduced network complexity, and increased network flexibility. By reducing the number of protocol messages exchanged between network devices, Segment Routing can also improve network performance, reducing latency and increasing throughput.

Information-Centric Networking (ICN), on the other hand, is an alternative networking paradigm that is focused on content rather than hosts or devices. ICN seeks to address some of the shortcomings of traditional networking architectures by enabling content-aware routing, caching, and delivery. In an ICN architecture, content is uniquely named and can be requested directly by clients, rather than by specifying the location of the host or server that contains the content. This approach can significantly reduce the number of hops required to access content, improving network performance and reducing latency.

The impact of these advanced network architecture concepts on network design and performance can be significant. For example, Segment Routing can enable more efficient network designs, where traffic is routed along pre-defined paths without requiring complex routing protocols. This can reduce the amount of hardware required to build the network and simplify network management.

Similarly, ICN can enable more efficient content delivery, with content being delivered directly to clients, rather than needing to traverse multiple network hops to reach its destination. This can reduce network congestion, improve performance, and reduce latency.

However, implementing these advanced network architecture concepts can also be complex and require significant changes to existing network designs and protocols. It is important to thoroughly evaluate the potential benefits and challenges before deploying these technologies in production networks.

6.3   Can you explain the concept of network automation through intent, and how it is applied in Intent-Based Networking (IBN) solutions?

Network automation through intent is a concept that seeks to simplify network management by enabling users to specify the desired outcome or intent of a network operation, rather than the specific steps to achieve it. Intent-Based Networking (IBN) solutions build on this idea by using automation and artificial intelligence (AI) to translate the user's intent into network configuration commands.

The intent describes the desired state of the network, such as "ensure that all mission-critical applications have at least 99

To enable this process, IBN solutions rely on a number of key technologies and principles. First, they use software-defined networking (SDN) to create a virtualized network infrastructure that can be managed centrally using automation and orchestration tools. This allows for rapid deployment and dynamic scaling of network resources as demand changes.

Secondly, IBN solutions typically incorporate machine learning and AI algorithms that analyze network traffic, user behavior, and other data sources to identify patterns and correlations. The algorithms can then make informed decisions about network operations and optimizations, and even predict potential problems before they occur.

Finally, IBN solutions use APIs and other interfaces to integrate with external systems and applications, such as cloud platforms or security systems. This ensures that the network is always aligned with the overall business objectives and requirements.

One example of the application of IBN is the use of Cisco's Application Centric Infrastructure (ACI) solution in a data center environment. With ACI, administrators can define the intent of the network, such as ensuring that a specific application always has enough bandwidth to operate efficiently. ACI then uses automation and policy-based management to configure the network infrastructure to achieve that goal.

In summary, network automation through intent and IBN solutions offer a powerful way to simplify network management, increase efficiency, and align network operations with business objectives. They represent an exciting and rapidly evolving area of computer networking that promises to change the way we design, implement, and operate our network infrastructures.

6.4   What are the key considerations and challenges in implementing and managing secure and scalable global backbone networks?

Implementing and managing a secure and scalable global backbone network can pose several challenges to network administrators. In this answer, we will discuss the key considerations and challenges involved in managing such networks.

Key considerations:

1. Network architecture: The backbone network architecture should be able to provide high availability, low latency, and high bandwidth to support data-intensive applications. There are several architectures to choose from, including point-to-point, multipoint, and mesh architectures.

2. Security: Backbone networks often carry sensitive data, so network security is a critical consideration. Security mechanisms like firewalls, intrusion detection systems, and virtual private networks (VPNs) need to be implemented to protect the network from external and internal threats.

3. Scalability: As the network grows, it is essential to ensure that the network is easily scalable. This includes having sufficient network resources to handle increased traffic loads, adding new sites and users without downtime, and implementing traffic engineering to optimize network performance.

4. Network management: A global backbone network requires a robust network management system to monitor network performance, troubleshoot issues, and manage resources. Network management systems should be able to support network automation, remote management, and network analytics.

Challenges:

1. Geographic diversity: A global backbone network spans across different geographies, making it challenging to manage. Different network technologies, protocols, and standards may be used in different regions, making it challenging to maintain a consistent network architecture.

2. Bandwidth constraints: Some regions may have limited bandwidth availability, which can impact network performance. Network administrators need to consider network traffic engineering to optimize traffic routing and manage bandwidth effectively.

3. Security threats: Global backbone networks are a lucrative target for cybercriminals, making network security a major challenge. Network administrators need to ensure that security policies are enforced and security mechanisms are in place to protect the network.

4. Cost: Building and maintaining a global backbone network can be expensive. Network administrators need to consider the cost of acquiring network equipment, deploying network infrastructure, and maintaining the network. Additionally, managing the network requires highly skilled network engineers, which can add to the cost.

In conclusion, implementing and managing a secure and scalable global backbone network requires careful consideration of network architecture, security, scalability, and network management. Network administrators also need to overcome challenges such as geographic diversity, bandwidth constraints, security threats, and cost.

6.5 Can you discuss the impact of emerging technologies like quantum computing and post-quantum cryptography on network security and infrastructure?

Quantum computing is a revolutionary technology which has massive implications for network security and infrastructure. It has the potential to break many of the encryption systems that we rely on today, including those used in most secure online transactions.

Post-quantum cryptography is a field that studies cryptographic algorithms (like encryption and digital signatures) which could still be secure against attacks by quantum computers. It is essential to develop post-quantum cryptography to ensure that our data remains secure even in the age of quantum computers.

When quantum computers become more widely available, several encryption algorithms currently in use today will become vulnerable to attacks. For example, the widely-used RSA algorithm depends on the fact that factoring large numbers is a difficult problem for classical computers. However, Shor's algorithm, which is a quantum algorithm, can factor large numbers much more quickly than classical algorithms. This means that if a quantum computer becomes powerful enough to implement Shor's algorithm, it would be able to break RSA encryption.

Providers of encrypted communication and storage, such as Google and Amazon Web Services, have already begun researching post-quantum cryptography solutions to prepare for the eventual arrival of quantum computers. NIST (National Institute of Standards and Technology) is also running a competition to standardize post-quantum cryptography algorithms.

Network infrastructure will also be impacted by quantum computing. For example, quantum networking, which uses quantum mechanics to transmit information, will offer faster and more secure methods of communication. It would also make it possible to create new methods of cryptography that rely on quantum mechanical principles.

In conclusion, emerging technologies like quantum computing and post-quantum cryptography will have a significant impact on network security and infrastructure. The development of post-quantum cryptography is essential to ensure that our data remains secure even in the age of quantum computers, and that new methods of cryptography can be explored. Quantum networking and new cryptographic methods will also likely emerge, and network infrastructure will need to adapt to these changes.

6.6   How do advanced network resource allocation and optimization techniques like Network Calculus help improve network performance and predictability?

Advanced network resource allocation and optimization techniques like Network Calculus are essential in improving network performance and predictability. Network Calculus is a mathematical theory used to model and analyze various aspects of network communication systems. It helps in developing systematic methods to ensure efficient network resource management.

One of the most significant benefits of Network Calculus is its ability to provide guaranteed performance bounds, which is essential in ensuring network predictability. For instance, it can provide upper bounds on end-to-end delays, packet loss probabilities, and buffer space requirements. These performance bounds help network engineers to design networks that meet the desired Quality of Service (QoS) requirements.

Another critical advantage of Network Calculus is its ability to analyze the end-to-end system performance. It considers the network's topology, buffer size, packet transmission rates, etc., to compute the end-to-end performance metrics, which help in identifying system bottlenecks and resource allocation issues. For example, if the network is congested due to a lack of resources, Network Calculus can help identify the optimal buffer sizes and rates of packet transmission to ensure smooth network operation.

Network Calculus also makes it possible to allocate network resources optimally. This is done by modeling the network as a set of service curves, which determine the amount of data that can be transmitted per unit time. By using Network Calculus, we can allocate resources such that the amount of data that can be transmitted is maximized while ensuring that the QoS requirements are met.

In summary, advanced network resource allocation and optimization techniques like Network Calculus help in improving network performance and predictability by providing performance bounds, analyzing end-to-end system performance, and optimal resource allocation.

6.7   What are the key aspects to consider when designing and implementing network architectures for ultra-low latency and high-reliability use cases, such as autonomous vehicles and smart cities?

Designing and implementing network architectures for ultra-low latency and high-reliability use cases, such as autonomous vehicles and smart cities, require careful consideration of several key aspects.

Firstly, the network architecture should prioritize low latency and high reliability. This means that the network should be designed to minimize delays in transferring data between devices and ensure that data is reliably transmitted and received without loss or corruption. To achieve this, the network should be designed using high-performance hardware and software components, and should incorporate redundancy and failover mechanisms to ensure continuous operation in the event of component failures.

Secondly, the network architecture should be scalable and flexible, able to support a large number of devices and data types, and be able to easily adapt to changing circumstances and requirements. For example, in the case of autonomous vehicles, the network architecture should be able to handle large volumes of data from sensors and other devices in real-time, while in smart cities, the network should be able to process and analyze data from many different sources to enable effective decision making.

Thirdly, security should be a key consideration in the design and implementation of the network architecture. Ultra-low latency and high-reliability use cases require sensitive and confidential data to be transmitted and received securely, so the network architecture should incorporate strong encryption and authentication measures to protect against unauthorized access and data breaches.

Fourthly, the network architecture should be designed with fault tolerance in mind. In use cases such as autonomous vehicles, failures in the network can have potentially catastrophic consequences. Therefore, the network should be designed to detect and mitigate faults automatically, ensuring high availability and minimizing the impact of any failures.

Finally, the network architecture should support quality of service (QoS) guarantees to ensure that critical traffic, such as control signals and emergency communications, receive priority treatment over less important traffic. This requires the network to be able to identify and prioritize traffic flows based on their importance, and to be able to allocate network resources accordingly.

In conclusion, designing and implementing network architectures for ultra-low latency and high-reliability use cases such as autonomous vehicles and smart cities requires careful consideration of several key aspects. These include prioritizing low latency and high reliability, scalability and flexibility, security, fault tolerance, and support for QoS guarantees.

6.8 Can you explain the role of network slicing in the context of multi-tenant and multi-service networks, and the challenges associated with its implementation and management?

Network slicing is a technique that allows the creation of multiple logical networks, using a single physical infrastructure. Each virtual network can provide a set of network functions and services that are customized to meet the specific requirements of a particular use case. In the context of multi-tenant and multi-service networks, network slicing enables the creation of dedicated virtual networks that are tailored to the needs of specific tenants or services.

In a multi-tenant network, network slicing can be used to isolate the traffic and services of different tenants, providing them with a dedicated virtual network environment that is secure, efficient and cost effective. For example, a service provider can use network slicing to create separate virtual networks for its different customers, providing them with dedicated bandwidth, quality of service (QoS) and security features that are customized to meet their specific needs. This enables service providers to offer differentiated services to their customers, while optimizing the utilization of their network resources.

In a multi-service network, network slicing can be used to support different types of services with varying requirements for bandwidth, QoS and latency. For example, a telecom operator can use network slicing to create separate virtual networks for each of its different services, such as voice, video, data and Internet of Things (IoT) applications. Each virtual network can provide different levels of performance and service quality, based on the specific requirements of each service. This enables telecom operators to offer a wide range of services with different pricing models, while ensuring the optimal utilization of their network resources.

However, the implementation and management of network slicing also pose significant challenges. One of the key challenges is the need for robust orchestration and management tools that can automate the creation, allocation and management of virtual network resources.

This requires a high degree of coordination between different network functions, such as software-defined networking (SDN), network functions virtualization (NFV), and cloud computing platforms.

Another challenge is the need for standardized, interoperable interfaces between different network functions and systems, to enable seamless integration of virtual networks across different domains and platforms. This requires the adoption of open standards and frameworks, such as the 3rd Generation Partnership Project (3GPP) and the Linux Foundation's Open Network Automation Platform (ONAP).

Finally, network slicing also raises important security and privacy concerns, as it involves the sharing of physical network resources among multiple virtual networks. Service providers must implement robust security measures and compliance frameworks to ensure that the data and services of different tenants and services are adequately protected, while maintaining the required levels of service quality and performance.

In conclusion, network slicing is a powerful technique that enables the creation of customized, dedicated virtual networks in multi-tenant and multi-service network environments. While it offers significant benefits in terms of service differentiation and resource optimization, it also poses significant challenges in terms of implementation, management and security. Addressing these challenges requires a collaborative and standards-based approach to network architecture and management.

6.9   How do advanced network resilience and fault-tolerance techniques like Byzantine Fault Tolerance (BFT) work, and when should they be considered?

Advanced network resilience and fault-tolerance techniques such as Byzantine Fault Tolerance (BFT) are designed to ensure that computer systems are able to continue operating in the face of failures and attacks, even when some of the components involved are unreliable or malicious. BFT is particularly useful for distributed systems where there is no single trusted authority or "centralized" control.

BFT works by combining several methods of achieving fault-tolerance, such as redundancy, replication, and voting-based decision-making. The basic idea behind BFT is to divide the system into multiple nodes or processes that work together to reach a consensus on the correct state of the system, even if some of the components are faulty or malicious. Byzantine refers to the concept of a traitorous or conflict of interest in a system with malicious nodes that would try to harm or disrupt the sharing of information.

One popular algorithm used for BFT is the Practical Byzantine Fault Tolerance algorithm (PBFT). PBFT requires that the number of nodes in the system be known and that a majority of them are functioning properly. The PBFT algorithm works by allowing the nodes in the network to send messages to each other to determine the state of the system. If a node receives a message from another node that disagrees with its own state, it will communicate with the other nodes to verify which state is correct. Each node validates the messages it receives from other nodes and agrees on a final decision through a voting method.

When considering BFT, it is necessary to balance the complexity of the system with the likelihood and severity of failures or attacks. BFT is typically used in situations where there is a significant risk of network failure or where the consequences of failure are severe, such as in financial applications or critical infrastructure. Organizations also often use BFT algorithms to supply decentralized and trustless applications using blockchain technologies. However, implementing BFT can be challenging due to the increased complexity and overhead, and there may be performance trade-offs to consider.

In summary, BFT is an advanced network resilience and fault-tolerance technique that uses redundancy, replication, and voting-based decision-making to ensure that a distributed system continues to function properly even in the presence of failures or attacks. While implementing BFT provides increased reliability, organizations should balance the complexity and potential performance trade-offs against the likelihood and consequences of failure.

6.10   What are the key challenges and solutions associated with ensuring end-to-end network security and privacy in an increasingly interconnected world?

Ensuring end-to-end network security and privacy is a critical challenge in the increasingly interconnected world. It involves preventing unauthorized access, eavesdropping, tampering, and data breaches. The key challenges and solutions associated with ensuring end-to-end network security and privacy are discussed below.

Challenges

Increasing complexity: As the network grows in size and complexity, it becomes more challenging to manage and secure. Therefore, the increasing complexity of network infrastructure poses challenges for security and privacy.

Distributed nature of modern applications: Modern applications deployed on the cloud are distributed and often span multiple organizations' networks. Therefore, securing this type of application is challenging due to its distributed nature.

Emergence of advanced threats: Cyber threats are continuously evolving, which makes it challenging to keep up with the latest threats and vulnerabilities.

Lack of security expertise: Organizations often lack security expertise, making it difficult to design, implement, and maintain secure networks.

Data privacy: Protecting privacy is becoming increasingly important, but it can be complicated to ensure data privacy in a connected world where data moves across and between networks.

Solutions

Implementing a defense-in-depth approach: This approach involves implementing multiple layers of security controls at different points in the network to increase overall security. For example, using firewalls, antivirus software, intrusion detection systems, and access controls.

Segmentation and isolation: Organizations can use techniques like network segmentation and isolation to minimize the scope of an attack. For example, creating a separate network for payment processing, thereby isolating it from other systems.

Employee education and training: Providing security training to employees can reduce security risks by making employees aware of best practices and security policies.

Data encryption: Encrypting sensitive data end-to-end can protect it from attackers who gain access to the network. By encrypting messages, they become indecipherable to anyone without the encryption key.

Implementing a comprehensive security policy: Organizations can create and enforce policies outlining cybersecurity best practices accepted by all team members to prevent data breaches, cyber attacks, and other malicious activities.

In conclusion, ensuring end-to-end network security and privacy is essential for maintaining trust and protecting assets, data, and privacy in our networked world. Organizations can achieve this using a combination of defense-in-depth approaches, network segmentation and isolation, employee education and training, data encryption, and implementing a comprehensive security policy.

6.11 Can you discuss the impact of emerging network technologies like Time-Sensitive Networking (TSN) and Deterministic Networking (DetNet) on real-time and mission-critical applications?

Emerging network technologies like Time-Sensitive Networking (TSN) and Deterministic Networking (DetNet) are designed to support real-time, mission-critical applications. TSN and DetNet both provide mechanisms to ensure that critical data is delivered within a prede-fined time window with minimal delay and jitter.

Time-Sensitive Networking is a set of IEEE standards that provide deterministic Quality of Service (QoS) for time-critical traffic in Eth-ernet networks. TSN uses a variety of mechanisms for scheduling and delaying network traffic, including time synchronization, traffic shaping, and admission control. By using TSN, network adminis-trators can guarantee QoS for applications that require high-speed, low-latency data transmission. For example, in industrial control ap-plications such as robotics, TSN can ensure that control signals are delivered within a precise time window, while video streams are de-livered with low delay and jitter.

Deterministic Networking (DetNet) is another emerging technology that provides deterministic QoS for mission-critical applications. Det-Net uses a combination of hops, flows, and paths to ensure that mission-critical data is delivered on time with minimal delay and jit-ter. DetNet supports a variety of applications, including industrial automation, power grid control, and autonomous vehicles. For exam-ple, in the aviation industry, DetNet can be used to ensure that data from sensors and control systems is delivered within a precise time window, while still allowing for the transmission of non-critical data like passenger entertainment systems.

Both TSN and DetNet are designed to ensure reliable, predictable packet delivery for real-time applications. As the number of IoT devices and real-time applications increases, networks will need to provide deterministic QoS to ensure that critical data is delivered within a precise time window. The impact of emerging technologies like TSN and DetNet on real-time and mission-critical applications is significant, as they provide the tools necessary to ensure reliable, secure, and fast packet delivery.

6.12 How do advanced network analysis and modeling techniques like stochastic network calculus and queuing theory help in network performance prediction and optimization?

Advanced network analysis and modeling techniques such as stochastic network calculus and queuing theory play a critical role in optimizing network performance. These techniques help network administrators understand network traffic behavior and predict future traffic patterns. By assessing traffic patterns, administrators can tune network parameters like buffer sizes and routing algorithms to improve network performance.

Stochastic network calculus is a mathematical framework that evaluates how the network can deliver data packets in a timely and reliable manner. It utilizes probability theory to create models that predict network traffic behavior. The theory is helpful when designing data networks characterized by queuing, delay, and packet loss. For instance, it is used to determine whether the network is congested under heavy traffic loads and whether packets will arrive at their destinations on time or not. The technique can also determine the amount of data lost during transmission such that measures to minimize packet loss can be taken.

Queuing theory is a mathematical framework used for analyzing the behavior of queue-based systems such as computer networks. It's used to model the performance of different network architectures, predict how long it takes to transmit data, and estimate the queue length. Queuing theory is vital in optimizing network performance since it enables network administrators to design networks with optimal size and capacity to handle network traffic.

Queuing theory provides a range of applicable models for analyzing network performance, such as $M/M/1$, $M/G/1$, $M/G/m$, etc. These models are used to analyze different network scenarios involving the mean arrival rate, response time, and processing time. Typically, based on the results of these models, network administrators can adjust network parameters to improve network performance.

In summary, advanced network analysis and modeling techniques such as stochastic network calculus and queuing theory help in network performance prediction and optimization by enabling network administrators to gain a better understanding of network behavior under different conditions, which presents the opportunity to fine-tune network parameters and optimize them for the best possible performance.

6.13 Can you explain the challenges and solutions associated with network function decomposition and disaggregation in the context of network virtualization and software-defined infrastructure?

Network function decomposition and disaggregation are critical concepts in the context of network virtualization and software-defined infrastructure. Network function decomposition is the process of breaking down network functions into smaller, more manageable elements. Disaggregation involves separating network hardware from software functions, allowing network administrators to modify and upgrade individual components rather than replacing entire systems. These concepts are essential to network virtualization and software-defined infrastructure as it helps to create more flexible networks that enable faster innovation and deployment of new network services.

However, while network function decomposition and disaggregation offer significant benefits, they also come with a variety of challenges that must be addressed. Some of the major challenges and their solutions are described below:

1. Integration and Interoperability: One of the biggest challenges associated with network function decomposition is integration and interoperability. As network functions are broken down into smaller components, ensuring that all these components work together effectively becomes more complex. This is particularly true when different vendors provide different components. To overcome this challenge, network administrators must ensure that all components are interop-

erable and capable of working together.

2. Performance: Another challenge associated with network function decomposition is performance. When network functions are broken down into smaller components, the system may experience reduced performance due to increased complexity. This can result in increased latency and reduced throughput. To overcome this challenge, network administrators must ensure that the system is designed to deliver optimal performance even with increased complexity.

3. Security: Network function disaggregation is also a potential security risk as separating network hardware from software functions can create vulnerabilities that can be exploited by attackers. To minimize this risk, network administrators must implement effective security measures such as firewalls, intrusion detection systems, and encryption to ensure that data is protected.

4. Scalability: Yet another challenge associated with network function disaggregation is scalability. As network functions are disaggregated and offered as individual services, it can be difficult to manage and scale the system effectively. To overcome this challenge, network administrators must ensure that the system is designed to scale easily and can handle the varying demands of different network services.

In conclusion, network function decomposition and disaggregation are essential concepts in the context of network virtualization and software-defined infrastructure. While they offer significant benefits, they also come with challenges such as integration and interoperability, performance, security, and scalability. By understanding these challenges and implementing effective solutions, network administrators can create more flexible and efficient networks that can adapt to evolving business needs.

6.14 What are the key aspects to consider when designing and implementing network architectures for energy-efficient and sustainable networking?

When designing and implementing network architectures for energy-efficient and sustainable networking, there are several key aspects that need to be considered. These aspects are network topology, protocols, and hardware. In this answer, I will explain each aspect in detail and provide examples to illustrate their importance.

1. Network Topology: The network topology is the physical or logical arrangement of nodes in a network. The network topology plays a crucial role in energy efficiency and sustainability as it determines the amount of energy required to transmit data between nodes. A well-designed network topology can reduce energy consumption and carbon footprint.

For example, a mesh network topology is preferred over a star network topology because in a mesh network, nodes can communicate directly with each other, reducing the number of hops required for data transmission. This reduces the amount of energy required and makes the network more energy-efficient. Another example is the use of hierarchical network topologies, where nodes are grouped together into levels, with each level representing a different function. This reduces the amount of energy required to transmit data between nodes, as data only needs to travel between nodes at the same level.

2. Protocols: Protocols are a set of rules and standards that govern communication between devices in a network. The use of energy-efficient protocols can significantly reduce energy consumption and create sustainable networking.

For example, the use of IPv6 over IPv4 can lead to energy savings as IPv6 is optimized for low power consumption in wireless networks. Another example is the Transmission Control Protocol (TCP), which optimizes data transmission by reducing the number of retransmissions required, thereby reducing energy consumption.

3. Hardware: The hardware used in a network plays a crucial role

in energy efficiency and sustainability. Energy-efficient hardware can significantly reduce energy consumption and create sustainable networking.

For example, the use of energy-efficient switches and routers that consume less power can significantly reduce energy consumption. Another example is the use of Energy Efficient Ethernet (EEE) technology, which dynamically adjusts the power consumption of network interfaces based on traffic load and link status.

In conclusion, designers and implementers of network architectures must consider the network topology, protocols, and hardware when designing for energy-efficient and sustainable networking. By optimizing each aspect, designers can create network architectures that consume less energy, reduce carbon footprint, and promote sustainable networking.

6.15   How do advanced network security techniques like moving target defense and network deception help protect against advanced persistent threats (APTs) and sophisticated attackers?

Advanced network security techniques such as Moving Target Defense (MTD) and Network Deception (ND) play a critical role in protecting against Advanced Persistent Threats (APTs) and sophisticated attackers.

MTD is a proactive approach that involves regularly changing the network and system configurations to make it difficult for attackers to find and exploit vulnerabilities. It achieves this by creating dynamic and unpredictable network environments that thwart an attacker's reconnaissance efforts. Essentially, MTD seeks to increase the attacker's cost of attack by reducing the effectiveness of their attack.

For example, MTD can involve continuously changing the IP addresses of various hosts, modifying configurations of network services, or even changing memory locations of critical system functions. By making these types of changes, the attacker is forced to constantly adapt and find new weaknesses, which requires time and effort, ultimately increasing the cost and reducing the effectiveness of their attack.

ND is another proactive approach that uses decoys or honeypots to attract attackers and divert them away from sensitive systems. It is essentially a form of deception that aims to mislead attackers and make it hard for them to distinguish between real and fake resources. ND can involve creating a wide range of decoy networks, endpoints, and services to make it more difficult for attackers to find and target the actual network resources.

For example, ND can be used to create a fake web server that appears real but is actually a decoy. When accessed by a potential attacker or a scanning tool, the fake server appears to be normal, but behind the scenes, it captures and logs all the activities, giving the security team valuable insight into the attacker's attack techniques.

MTD and ND can complement each other and provide a more comprehensive approach to threat mitigation. By using MTD to continuously change the network environment and ND to mislead attackers, it becomes significantly more difficult for attackers to successfully carry out an APT attack.

In summary, MTD and ND provide highly effective methods of combating APTs by making it difficult for attackers to identify and exploit vulnerabilities. Incorporating these advanced techniques into network security infrastructures provides a powerful defense against today's highly advanced and persistent attackers.

6.16   Can you discuss the role of inter-domain routing and peering in the context of large-scale Internet infrastructure, and the challenges and solutions associated with it?

Inter-domain routing and peering are essential components of large-scale Internet infrastructure.

Inter-domain routing refers to the process of exchanging traffic between different Autonomous Systems (ASes) that form the internet. An Autonomous System is a group of interconnected networks that operate under a common administrative domain. Inter-domain routing is typically performed by routers using the Border Gateway Protocol (BGP), which is the de-facto standard protocol for inter-domain routing.

Peering is a voluntary agreement between two or more networks to exchange traffic directly between their networks without going through a third-party transit provider. This is typically done to save on costs associated with transit providers and to improve performance by reducing the number of hops between endpoints. Peering is usually done through physical interconnections at Internet Exchange Points (IXPs) or through virtual interconnections known as peering sessions.

One of the biggest challenges associated with inter-domain routing and peering is ensuring that traffic is efficiently routed across multiple ASes to reach its destination. This can be particularly difficult in the face of dynamic network conditions, changing traffic patterns, and the complexity of the routing system.

Another challenge is negotiating and maintaining peering agreements. Peering agreements can be complex and time-consuming to negotiate, and they require ongoing maintenance and monitoring to ensure that both parties are adhering to the agreement and that the peering relationship is beneficial to both parties.

To address these challenges, a number of solutions have been developed. These include the deployment of more sophisticated routing protocols and technologies, such as Multiprotocol Label Switching

(MPLS) and Software-Defined Networking (SDN), which can help to improve the efficiency and flexibility of the routing system. Additionally, the development of standards and best practices for peering, such as the Mutually Agreed Norms for Routing Security (MANRS), can help to improve the stability and security of inter-domain routing and peering relationships.

In conclusion, inter-domain routing and peering are essential components of large-scale Internet infrastructure, and they present both challenges and solutions. As the internet continues to grow and evolve, it is likely that we will see further advancements in routing and peering technologies and practices to ensure the continued stability, security, and efficiency of the network.

6.17   What are the key challenges and solutions in designing and implementing network infrastructures for extreme-scale and exascale computing environments?

Extreme-scale and exascale computing refer to the computational power needed to perform complex and large-scale scientific computing and data analysis. These computing environments require a robust and scalable network infrastructure that can meet the high-bandwidth and low-latency demands of the applications running on them. There are several challenges associated with designing and implementing network infrastructures for extreme-scale and exascale computing environments, some of which are discussed below:

Bandwidth: Extreme-scale and exascale computing environments generate massive amounts of data that must be transferred across the network at high speeds. The network infrastructure must be designed to handle the high-bandwidth demands of applications running on these systems. This can be achieved by using high-speed links, such as InfiniBand, that provide low-latency, high-bandwidth interconnectivity between the nodes of the system.

Scalability: Extreme-scale and exascale systems can comprise millions of compute nodes, which can pose a significant challenge when designing a network infrastructure. The network must be scalable to accommodate the increasing number of nodes in the system, and it must provide efficient communication between these nodes. One solution is to use a hierarchical network topology, where nodes are organized in clusters, and these clusters are then connected to each other using a high-speed interconnect.

Topology: The network topology used in extreme-scale and exascale computing environments must be carefully designed to achieve low-latency and high-bandwidth connectivity between the compute nodes. A common approach is to use a fat-tree topology, where each node is connected to multiple switches, and these switches are then connected to higher-level switches until a single root switch is reached. This topology provides high-bandwidth connectivity between nodes and ensures that data can be transmitted efficiently across the network.

Power consumption: Large-scale systems consume a lot of power, and the network infrastructure must be designed to minimize power consumption while still providing high-performance connectivity. One solution is to use network components that are energy-efficient, such as low-power switches and cables.

Fault tolerance: With millions of nodes in the system, it is inevitable that some nodes or network components will fail. The network must be designed to provide fault-tolerant connectivity between the nodes, ensuring that data can still be transmitted even in the event of a failure. This can be achieved by using redundant network paths, so if one path fails, data can still be transmitted across an alternative path.

In conclusion, designing and implementing network infrastructures for extreme-scale and exascale computing environments involves a range of challenges, including bandwidth, scalability, topology, power consumption, and fault tolerance. To overcome these challenges, a range of solutions have been proposed, including using high-speed links, hierarchical network topologies, energy-efficient components, and redundant network paths.

6.18   How do advanced network management techniques like autonomic networking and self-healing networks help improve network performance, resilience, and adaptability?

Advanced network management techniques like autonomic networking and self-healing networks help improve network performance, resilience, and adaptability by enabling networks to monitor and manage themselves without human intervention.

Autonomic networking is an approach to network management that allows networks to self-configure, self-monitor, self-heal, and self-optimize. This means that the network can automatically detect and resolve issues without the need for human intervention. For instance, if a link in the network fails, the autonomic network would automatically reroute traffic to a different path to ensure that communication remains uninterrupted.

Self-healing networks are a type of autonomic network that is specifically designed to quickly recover from failures. For instance, when a device fails, the network can automatically identify the cause of the problem, isolate the failed device, and reroute traffic around the problem. This helps prevent data loss and minimize downtime.

Both autonomic networking and self-healing networks can also improve network performance by optimizing network resources, such as bandwidth and routing. For example, an autonomic network could detect that a particular application is consuming a large amount of bandwidth and automatically adjust the network configuration to allocate more bandwidth to the application. This improves overall network performance and ensures that critical applications are given the resources they need to function properly.

In addition, these techniques also improve network adaptability by allowing the network to respond to changing traffic patterns or demands. For instance, if the network is experiencing heavy traffic, it can adjust its resources to ensure that all traffic flows are prioritized and delivered efficiently.

Overall, advanced network management techniques like autonomic networking and self-healing networks can significantly improve network performance, resilience, and adaptability by automating network management and ensuring that networks can quickly identify and resolve issues without human intervention.

6.19 Can you discuss the impact of network convergence and the integration of heterogeneous networks, such as optical, wireless, and satellite networks, on network design and management?

The convergence of different network types, such as optical, wireless, and satellite networks, has led to significant changes in network design and management. This convergence has allowed for the creation of more complex and sophisticated networks that can offer a wider range of services and functionalities. In this answer, we will discuss the impact of network convergence and the integration of heterogeneous networks on network design and management.

One of the main impacts of network convergence is the need for networks to support multiple types of traffic, including voice, data, and video, over a single physical infrastructure. This requires a higher level of network scalability and reliability, as well as the ability to prioritize different types of traffic. For example, a converged network might prioritize voice traffic over data traffic to ensure that phone calls are not dropped.

Another impact of network convergence is the need for network administrators to have a greater understanding of different network technologies and protocols. This is necessary in order to ensure that all devices on the network can communicate with one another, regardless of the type of network they are using. For example, a network administrator may need to understand both wireless networking protocols (such as Wi-Fi) and optical networking protocols (such as Fiber Channel) in order to properly configure a converged network.

In addition, network convergence and the integration of heterogeneous networks has also led to a greater emphasis on network security. With multiple types of traffic traveling over the same physical infrastructure, it is critical to ensure that data is kept secure and protected from unauthorized access. This requires implementing stronger authentication and encryption mechanisms and using advanced security tools to prevent attacks.

Overall, the integration of different types of networks has significantly impacted network design and management. The convergence of different networks requires greater scalability, reliability, and security, as well as a greater understanding of different networking technologies and protocols. As networks continue to evolve and converge, it will be important for network administrators to stay up-to-date with the latest advancements in network design and management to ensure that their networks remain secure and reliable.

6.20   What are the emerging trends and research directions in computer networking, and how do they impact the future of network design, management, and security?

Emerging trends and research directions in computer networking are shaping the future of network design, management, and security. In this answer, I will discuss some of the notable trends and research directions and their impact on network technologies.

1. Internet of Things (IoT): IoT is the network of physical devices, vehicles, and other objects that are embedded with sensors, software, and network connectivity, enabling them to collect and exchange data. IoT is expected to have a significant impact on various industries, including healthcare, transportation, and manufacturing. However, IoT presents new challenges in terms of network design, management, and security. The massive number of IoT devices and the data they generate make it difficult to manage and secure the network. Furthermore, IoT devices may have limited processing power and memory,

making it challenging to implement security measures. Researchers are exploring new approaches to network architecture, security, and management to overcome these challenges.

2. Software-Defined Networking (SDN): SDN is an emerging networking paradigm that separates the network control plane from the data plane. SDN provides a centralized management and control of the network, making it easier to manage and automate network operations. SDN is being adopted by service providers and enterprises to simplify network management and orchestration. However, SDN also presents new challenges, such as the need for secure control communication, and efficient control placement. Researchers are investigating new architectures, protocols, and algorithms to overcome these challenges.

3. Blockchain: Blockchain is a decentralized, tamper-proof, and transparent ledger technology that is being applied to various use cases, including payment systems and supply chain management. Blockchain has the potential to improve network security by providing a decentralized and immutable record of network transactions. Research is being conducted to explore the use of blockchain for network security, authentication, and authorization. For instance, blockchain can be used to create a decentralized authentication system that eliminates the need for centralized identity providers.

4. Artificial Intelligence (AI) and Machine Learning (ML): AI and ML are being applied to various applications, including computer networking. AI can be used to automate network management tasks, such as traffic engineering, fault detection, and diagnosis. ML can be used to create predictive models of network performance and security, enabling proactive network operations. Research is being conducted to explore the use of AI and ML in network management and security, including the development of new algorithms and architectures.

In conclusion, the emerging trends and research directions in computer networking are shaping the future of network design, management, and security. Researchers are exploring new approaches to network architecture, security, and management to overcome the challenges presented by these trends. The impact of these trends on the network technologies is expected to be significant, and businesses and organizations must prepare themselves for these changes to remain competitive.

www.ingramcontent.com/pod-product-compliance
Lightning Source LLC
LaVergne TN
LVHW051343050326
832903LV00031B/3717